Preface

Java has remained one of the most widely used programming languages in the software industry, with applications ranging from enterprise solutions to web development, mobile applications, and cloud computing. As technology evolves, so do the expectations from Java developers. Companies today seek professionals who possess not only a strong foundation in Java but also expertise in advanced topics such as multithreading, design patterns, performance optimization, microservices, and frameworks like Spring and Hibernate.

This book, "Advanced Java Interview Questions & Answers", has been meticulously crafted to help developers and job seekers prepare for Java interviews with confidence. It serves as a comprehensive guide, covering a broad spectrum of advanced Java concepts that are frequently asked in technical interviews. Whether you are a fresher aiming to break into the industry or an experienced developer looking to level up your career, this book will be your go-to resource.

Each chapter presents interview questions along with detailed explanations, practical code snippets, and best practices to help you understand the underlying concepts. The questions are structured to reflect real-world problems faced by developers, enabling you to approach interviews with a problem-solving mindset. Additionally, we have included case studies and scenario-based questions to simulate real interview experiences.

Our goal is not only to help you crack interviews but also to enhance your Java expertise by reinforcing your knowledge of core and advanced concepts. We encourage you to practice the examples, experiment with code, and explore the additional resources provided in this book.

We hope this book serves as a valuable companion in your Java career journey. Happy learning and best of luck with your interviews!

TABLE OF CONTENT

CHAPTER 1
Network Basics and Socket Overview

1.1 Socket Communication

Question: What is the difference between Socket and DatagramSocket?
Answer: Socket is used for TCP-based communication, while DatagramSocket is used for UDP-based communication.

Question: What is a secure socket in Java?
Answer: A secure socket uses SSL/TLS for encrypted communication, implemented using the SSLSocket class.

Question: What is the role of the bind() method in socket communication?
Answer: It binds the socket to a specific local address and port.

Question: How do you implement authentication in socket communication?
Answer: Use a handshake protocol to exchange credentials during the connection setup phase.

Question: What is the difference between a server socket and a client socket?
Answer: A server socket listens for incoming connections, while a client socket initiates a connection to the server.

Question: How do you implement a multi-threaded server in Java?
Answer: Use a thread pool or create a new thread for each client connection.

Question: How do you send an object over a socket?
Answer: Use ObjectOutputStream to serialize and send the object.

Question: What is the role of flush() in socket communication?
Answer: It forces any buffered output bytes to be written out to the underlying stream.

Question: How can you retrieve the hostname of a client connected to a server?
Answer: Use the getInetAddress().getHostName() method of the client socket.

Question: What is the difference between a half-close and full-close in sockets?
Answer: A half-close allows one direction of communication to remain open, while a full-close terminates both directions.

Question: How do you enable KeepAlive for a socket in Java?
Answer: Use the setKeepAlive(true) method on the socket.

Question: What is a DatagramSocket used for?
Answer: A DatagramSocket is used for sending and receiving packets in a connectionless UDP communication.

Question: How do you parse a URL in socket communication?
Answer: Use the URL class to extract components like protocol, host, port, and path.

Question: What is the maximum number of concurrent connections a server socket can handle?
Answer: It depends on system resources and the backlog value specified when creating the server socket.

Question: How do you create a secure server socket in Java?
Answer: Use SSLServerSocketFactory to create an SSLServerSocket.

Question: How do you monitor active socket connections?
Answer: Maintain a list of active sockets on the server and log each connection.

Question: What is the purpose of the toString() method in a socket?
Answer: It provides a string representation of the socket's address and port.

Question: How do you detect socket disconnection?
Answer: Monitor the return value of the read() method, which returns -1 when the connection is closed.

Question: What is a timeout exception in socket communication?
Answer: A SocketTimeoutException is thrown when a read or connect operation exceeds the specified timeout.

Question: How do you implement load balancing for socket servers?
Answer: Use a load balancer or implement custom logic to distribute client requests across multiple servers.

Question: What is the role of the shutdownInput() and shutdownOutput() methods?
Answer: These methods partially close the input or output stream of a socket for half-duplex communication.

1.2 TCP/IP Client Sockets with Socket

Question: How do you create a TCP client socket in Java?
Answer: Instantiate the Socket class by specifying the server's hostname and port number, e.g., Socket socket = new Socket("localhost", 8080).

Question: What is the purpose of the getOutputStream() method in a client socket?
Answer: The getOutputStream() method retrieves the output stream to send data to the server.

Question: How does a TCP client socket communicate with a server?
Answer: It connects to the server, sends data using the output stream, and receives responses through the input stream.

Question: What happens if the server is unavailable when a client socket attempts to connect?
Answer: A ConnectException is thrown, indicating that the connection to the server failed.

Question: How do you set a timeout for a TCP client socket in Java?
Answer: Use the setSoTimeout(int timeout) method to set a timeout for socket operations.

Question: What is the difference between Socket and ServerSocket?
Answer: Socket is used for client-side connections, while ServerSocket is used to listen for incoming connections on the server side.

Question: How do you handle exceptions in TCP client socket communication?
Answer: Use try-catch blocks to handle IOException and SocketTimeoutException.

Question: What is the role of the close() method in client sockets?
Answer: The close() method releases resources and terminates the connection between the client and server.

Question: How can a TCP client socket detect the server's IP address?
Answer: Use the InetAddress class or call socket.getInetAddress().getHostAddress() to retrieve the server's IP.

Question: How do you send a string message to a server using a client socket?
Answer: Use the OutputStream wrapped in a PrintWriter, e.g., new PrintWriter(socket.getOutputStream(), true).println("Hello Server").

Question: How do you read a server's response in a client socket?

Answer: Use the InputStream with a BufferedReader, e.g., BufferedReader br = new BufferedReader(new InputStreamReader(socket.getInputStream())).

Question: What is the significance of port numbers in TCP client sockets?
Answer: Port numbers identify the specific service or process on the server the client wants to communicate with.

Question: How do you implement secure communication using client sockets?
Answer: Use SSLSocket for encrypted communication over SSL/TLS.

Question: Can a single client socket communicate with multiple servers?
Answer: No, a single socket instance can connect to one server. To communicate with multiple servers, create separate socket instances.

Question: How do you test a TCP client socket application?
Answer: Use tools like Telnet, Netcat, or create a mock server to simulate server-side behavior.

Question: What is the role of the isConnected() method in a client socket?
Answer: It checks whether the socket is currently connected to the server.

Question: How can you optimize TCP client socket performance?
Answer: Use buffered streams and ensure timely resource release by closing the socket and streams.

Question: How do you enable KeepAlive for a client socket?
Answer: Use socket.setKeepAlive(true) to maintain the connection even during periods of inactivity.

Question: What happens if the server sends data beyond what the client expects?
Answer: The extra data remains in the input buffer, and the client must handle it using appropriate reading mechanisms.

Question: How do you detect if the connection to the server is lost?
Answer: Monitor exceptions like SocketException or check if the read() method returns -1.

1.3 TCP/IP Server Sockets

Question: What is the purpose of a ServerSocket in Java?
Answer: A ServerSocket listens for incoming client connections and establishes a communication channel when a client connects.

Question: How do you create a TCP server socket in Java?
Answer: Instantiate a ServerSocket with a specific port, e.g., ServerSocket server = new ServerSocket(8080).

Question: How does a server accept a client connection?
Answer: Use the accept() method of the ServerSocket class to block and wait for an incoming connection.

Question: What is the role of the port number in a ServerSocket?
Answer: The port number specifies the application or service the server socket will listen to for incoming requests.

Question: How do you handle multiple client connections on a server socket?
Answer: Use multithreading to spawn a new thread for each client connection accepted by the server.

Question: What happens if the port used by a ServerSocket is already occupied?
Answer: A BindException is thrown, indicating the port is already in use.

Question: How do you specify a backlog for a server socket?

Answer: Pass the backlog value as the second parameter when creating the ServerSocket, e.g., new ServerSocket(8080, 50);.

Question: How do you close a server socket in Java?
Answer: Call the close() method on the ServerSocket instance to release the resources.

Question: What is the purpose of the getLocalPort() method in a server socket?
Answer: It retrieves the port number the server socket is bound to.

Question: How do you detect the IP address of a connected client?
Answer: Use the getInetAddress() method of the Socket object returned by accept().

Question: What exception is thrown if a ServerSocket times out waiting for a connection?
Answer: A SocketTimeoutException is thrown if a timeout is set using the setSoTimeout() method.

Question: How do you enable timeouts on a server socket?
Answer: Use the setSoTimeout(int timeout) method to specify the timeout duration in milliseconds.

Question: How do you send data from a server to a client?
Answer: Use the OutputStream of the Socket object returned by the accept() method to send data.

Question: How does a server read data from a client?
Answer: Use the InputStream of the Socket object returned by the accept() method to read data.

Question: What is the significance of the bind() method in server sockets?
Answer: The bind() method binds the server socket to a specific IP address and port.

Question: How can you implement secure communication on a server socket?
Answer: Use SSLServerSocket to enable encrypted communication using SSL/TLS protocols.

Question: What happens if a client disconnects abruptly?
Answer: The server socket will not be affected, but the Socket instance for the client may throw an IOException.

Question: How do you limit the number of concurrent connections to a server socket?
Answer: Use the backlog parameter during server socket creation or implement connection-limiting logic in the server code.

Question: How do you handle exceptions in server socket operations?
Answer: Use try-catch blocks to handle IOException and other relevant exceptions like BindException.

Question: What is the difference between ServerSocket and Socket?
Answer: ServerSocket listens for incoming connections, while Socket represents an established connection with a client.

1.4 InetAddress

Question: What is the purpose of the InetAddress class in Java?
Answer: The InetAddress class represents an IP address and provides methods to resolve hostnames to IP addresses and vice versa.

Question: How do you get the IP address of a hostname using InetAddress?
Answer: Use InetAddress.getByName("hostname").getHostAddress() to get the IP address of the specified hostname.

Question: How can you retrieve the hostname of an IP address?

Answer: Use the InetAddress.getByName("IP").getHostName() method to get the hostname for the specified IP address.

Question: What is the difference between getByName() and getByAddress() in InetAddress?
Answer: getByName() resolves a hostname to an IP address, while getByAddress() creates an InetAddress object using a byte array representing the IP address.

Question: How do you get the local host's IP address in Java?
Answer: Use InetAddress.getLocalHost().getHostAddress() to retrieve the local machine's IP address.

Question: What exception does InetAddress.getByName() throw?
Answer: It throws an UnknownHostException if the specified hostname cannot be resolved.

Question: How do you check if an InetAddress object represents a loopback address?
Answer: Use the isLoopbackAddress() method to check if the IP address is a loopback address (e.g., 127.0.0.1).

Question: What is the significance of the isReachable() method in InetAddress?
Answer: The isReachable(int timeout) method checks if the IP address is reachable within the specified timeout.

Question: How do you create an InetAddress object for a specific IP address?
Answer: Use InetAddress.getByAddress(byte[] ipAddress) to create an InetAddress object for the given IP address.

Question: How can you retrieve all IP addresses associated with a hostname?
Answer: Use InetAddress.getAllByName("hostname") to get an array of InetAddress objects representing all associated IPs.

Question: How does InetAddress support IPv6 addresses?
Answer: The InetAddress class supports both IPv4 and IPv6 addresses, and methods like getHostAddress() return the correct format.

Question: What is the role of getCanonicalHostName() in InetAddress?
Answer: The getCanonicalHostName() method returns the fully qualified domain name (FQDN) for the IP address.

Question: Can an InetAddress object represent multiple IP addresses?
Answer: No, a single InetAddress object represents one IP address, but getAllByName() can return multiple IPs for a hostname.

Question: How do you check if an IP address is a multicast address?
Answer: Use the isMulticastAddress() method to check if the address belongs to a multicast group.

Question: How does InetAddress handle DNS caching?
Answer: InetAddress uses DNS caching, and the cache behavior is controlled by system properties like networkaddress.cache.ttl.

Question: How do you obtain a wildcard address in InetAddress?
Answer: Use InetAddress.getByName("0.0.0.0") to get the wildcard address, which represents all available network interfaces.

Question: How do you differentiate between a public and private IP using InetAddress?
Answer: You need to parse the IP address manually and compare it against known private IP ranges, as InetAddress does not provide a direct method.

Question: How can you use InetAddress to check internet connectivity?

Answer: Use InetAddress.getByName("google.com").isReachable(timeout) to check if an external website is reachable.

Question: What is the significance of toString() in InetAddress?
Answer: The toString() method returns a string representation of the InetAddress object, combining the hostname and IP address.

Question: How do you test the equality of two InetAddress objects?
Answer: Use the equals() method to compare two InetAddress objects for equality based on their IP addresses.

1.5 URLs and URLConnection

Question: What is a URL in Java networking?
Answer: A URL (Uniform Resource Locator) represents the address of a resource on the internet and is handled by the java.net.URL class.

Question: How do you create a URL object in Java?
Answer: Use the URL constructor, e.g., URL url = new URL("http://example.com");.

Question: What are the key components of a URL?
Answer: A URL consists of the protocol, host, port (optional), and file (resource path).

Question: How do you retrieve the protocol of a URL?
Answer: Use the getProtocol() method, e.g., url.getProtocol().

Question: How do you retrieve the hostname of a URL?
Answer: Use the getHost() method, e.g., url.getHost().

Question: What is the purpose of the URLConnection class in Java?
Answer: The URLConnection class represents a communication link between a Java application and a URL resource.

Question: How do you open a connection to a URL in Java?
Answer: Use the openConnection() method of the URL class, e.g., URLConnection connection = url.openConnection();.

Question: How can you set a timeout for a URLConnection?
Answer: Use the setConnectTimeout(int timeout) and setReadTimeout(int timeout) methods.

Question: How do you read data from a URL using URLConnection?
Answer: Use the InputStream from the URLConnection object to read data, e.g., connection.getInputStream().

Question: How do you retrieve the content type of a URL resource?
Answer: Use the getContentType() method of the URLConnection object.

Question: What is the difference between HttpURLConnection and URLConnection?
Answer: HttpURLConnection is a subclass of URLConnection that provides methods specific to HTTP requests.

Question: How do you send a GET request using HttpURLConnection?
Answer: Set the request method to "GET" using setRequestMethod("GET") and then read the response.

Question: How do you send a POST request using HttpURLConnection?
Answer: Set the request method to "POST," enable output with setDoOutput(true), and write data to the OutputStream.

Question: How can you retrieve the response code from an HTTP connection?

Answer: Use the getResponseCode() method of the HttpURLConnection object.

Question: How do you check if a URL points to a file or directory?
Answer: Parse the URL path and check for a trailing slash or use specific server metadata if available.

Question: How do you handle redirections in HttpURLConnection?
Answer: Set setInstanceFollowRedirects(true) to allow automatic handling of redirections.

Question: What is the purpose of the toExternalForm() method in the URL class?
Answer: It converts the URL object to its external form as a string.

Question: How do you encode and decode URL parameters in Java?
Answer: Use URLEncoder.encode() to encode and URLDecoder.decode() to decode parameters.

Question: What is the significance of the getDefaultPort() method in a URL?
Answer: It returns the default port for the protocol specified in the URL.

Question: How do you handle an UnknownHostException when working with URL?
Answer: Handle it in a try-catch block to manage cases where the hostname cannot be resolved.

Online Resources

	Practice Paper	YouTube Video Playlist Link
Link	https://forms.gle/p1ZvDdS6PGg7WSpg8	https://www.youtube.com/playlist?list=PLzlh_31VWEFrVCJw3kRCEX-irsYWE6lxR
QR Code		

CHAPTER 2
JDBC Programming

2.1 The JDBC Connectivity Model

Question: What is the purpose of the setFetchSize() method in JDBC?
Answer: The setFetchSize() method specifies the number of rows to fetch from the database in a single round trip.

Question: How do you use savepoints in JDBC?
Answer: Use the setSavepoint() method to mark a point in a transaction and rollback(Savepoint savepoint) to roll back to it.

Question: What is the purpose of DatabaseMetaData in JDBC?
Answer: DatabaseMetaData provides information about the database, such as its capabilities, tables, and drivers.

Question: What is the use of the getGeneratedKeys() method?
Answer: The getGeneratedKeys() method retrieves auto-generated keys (like primary keys) after an INSERT operation.

Question: What are row sets in JDBC?
Answer: Row sets are enhanced ResultSet objects that support features like disconnected operation and serialization.

Question: How do you perform a batch update in JDBC?
Answer: Add multiple SQL statements using addBatch() and execute them using executeBatch().

Question: What is the difference between commit() and rollback()?
Answer: commit() saves changes made in a transaction, while rollback() reverts changes.

Question: How do you check if a connection is valid in JDBC?
Answer: Use the isValid(int timeout) method of the Connection interface.

Question: What is the use of rowId in JDBC?
Answer: RowId represents a unique identifier for a row in the database and can be retrieved using getRowId().

Question: What is a Scrollable ResultSet?
Answer: A Scrollable ResultSet allows you to navigate forward and backward through the query results.

Question: How do you retrieve metadata about a ResultSet?
Answer: Use the getMetaData() method of the ResultSet object.

Question: What are the different types of statements in JDBC?
Answer: The types are Statement, PreparedStatement, and CallableStatement.

Question: How do you update data in a ResultSet?
Answer: Use ResultSet methods like updateString(), updateInt(), and updateRow() to modify data.

Question: What is connection pooling in JDBC?
Answer: Connection pooling is a technique to reuse database connections for better performance and resource management.

Question: How does JDBC support batch processing?
Answer: JDBC supports batch processing using the addBatch() and executeBatch() methods for bulk updates.

Question: How do you execute stored procedures in JDBC?
Answer: Use CallableStatement to execute stored procedures.

Question: What is the role of ParameterMetaData in JDBC?
Answer: ParameterMetaData provides information about parameters in a PreparedStatement.

Question: How can you retrieve database-specific keywords in JDBC?
Answer: Use the getSQLKeywords() method of the DatabaseMetaData object.

Question: How do you handle large binary data in JDBC?
Answer: Use Blob for binary data and Clob for large text data.

Question: What is JDBC 4.0's feature for auto-loading drivers?
Answer: In JDBC 4.0 and later, drivers are auto-loaded at runtime without explicitly calling Class.forName().

2.2 Creating a SQL Query

Question: How do you retrieve data from a SELECT query in JDBC?
Answer: Use ResultSet methods like next(), getString(), or getInt() to retrieve and process data row by row.

Question: How do you optimize performance when creating SQL queries in Java?
Answer: Use PreparedStatement for repeated queries, index database columns, and limit fetched rows.

Question: How do you handle null values in a SQL query?
Answer: Use IS NULL in the query or check for null in the application code before processing the data.

Question: What is the purpose of the setMaxRows() method in JDBC?
Answer: The setMaxRows() method limits the number of rows returned by a query.

Question: How do you use JOINs in a SQL query in JDBC?
Answer: Include JOIN clauses in the SQL query string and execute it using Statement or PreparedStatement.

Question: How do you perform a query with ORDER BY in JDBC?
Answer: Add an ORDER BY clause to the SQL query string before executing it.

Question: How do you perform a query with GROUP BY in JDBC?
Answer: Add a GROUP BY clause to the SQL query string and process the aggregated results using ResultSet.

Question: How do you perform a query with WHERE conditions in JDBC?
Answer: Add a WHERE clause to filter rows and use placeholders (?) for dynamic parameters.

Question: How do you use aggregate functions in a SQL query in JDBC?
Answer: Include aggregate functions like SUM(), COUNT(), AVG(), etc., in the query string.

Question: What is the significance of the LIMIT clause in a SQL query?
Answer: The LIMIT clause restricts the number of rows returned by a query, improving performance.

Question: How do you perform a query with a subquery in JDBC?
Answer: Include a subquery within the main SQL query string and execute it using Statement or PreparedStatement.

Question: What is the role of the LIKE operator in SQL queries?
Answer: The LIKE operator is used for pattern matching in WHERE conditions.

Question: How do you execute a query with a HAVING clause in JDBC?
Answer: Add a HAVING clause to filter aggregated results and execute the query as usual.

Question: How do you combine queries using UNION in JDBC?
Answer: Construct a query with the UNION operator and execute it using Statement or PreparedStatement.

Question: How do you handle special characters in SQL queries?
Answer: Escape special characters or use PreparedStatement to avoid issues like SQL injection.

Question: What is the purpose of the DISTINCT keyword in SQL queries?
Answer: The DISTINCT keyword removes duplicate rows from the query results.

Question: How do you update multiple rows in a SQL query?
Answer: Use an UPDATE query with a WHERE condition that matches multiple rows.

Question: How do you delete rows using a SQL query in JDBC?
Answer: Use a DELETE statement with a WHERE condition and execute it using executeUpdate().

Question: How do you insert multiple rows in a SQL query?
Answer: Use a single INSERT statement with multiple values or batch processing for better performance.

Question: How do you create a table using a SQL query in JDBC?
Answer: Use a CREATE TABLE statement and execute it using the execute() method.

2.3 Getting the Results

Question: What is the default cursor behavior of a ResultSet?
Answer: By default, a ResultSet is TYPE_FORWARD_ONLY and read-only.

Question: What is the difference between relative(int rows) and absolute(int row) in ResultSet?
Answer: relative() moves the cursor relative to its current position, while absolute() moves it to an absolute row number.

Question: How do you check the type of a ResultSet?
Answer: Use the getType() method to determine if the ResultSet is forward-only or scrollable.

Question: Can you navigate a ResultSet without rows?
Answer: No, attempting to navigate a ResultSet with no rows will cause the cursor methods to return false.

Question: How do you retrieve a timestamp from a ResultSet?
Answer: Use the getTimestamp() method to retrieve a SQL TIMESTAMP value.

Question: What is the getConcurrency() method in ResultSet?
Answer: The getConcurrency() method returns the concurrency mode of the ResultSet, such as CONCUR_READ_ONLY or CONCUR_UPDATABLE.

Question: How do you close a ResultSet in JDBC?
Answer: Call the close() method to release resources associated with the ResultSet.

Question: How do you check for duplicate rows in a ResultSet?
Answer: Use custom logic, such as comparing values programmatically while iterating through the rows.

Question: Can you combine multiple ResultSet objects?
Answer: No, but you can merge their data programmatically by iterating through both.

Question: How do you retrieve data from an alias column in a ResultSet?
Answer: Use the alias name in the get methods to retrieve the value.

Question: How do you retrieve a date value from a ResultSet?
Answer: Use the getDate() method to retrieve a DATE value.

Question: What happens if the cursor moves beyond the last row in a ResultSet?
Answer: The next() method returns false, indicating no more rows.

Question: How do you retrieve multiple rows using a ResultSet?
Answer: Use a loop with the next() method to iterate through each row.

Question: What is the use of the first() method in ResultSet?
Answer: The first() method moves the cursor to the first row in a scrollable ResultSet.

Question: How do you get column data by column index in ResultSet?
Answer: Use getString(int columnIndex) or similar methods, providing the column index.

Question: How do you check the number of rows in a ResultSet?
Answer: Iterate through the ResultSet while counting rows or use SQL to count rows directly.

Question: How do you retrieve a floating-point value from a ResultSet?
Answer: Use the getFloat() or getDouble() methods to retrieve floating-point values.

Question: What happens if you call ResultSet.getString() on a non-string column?
Answer: The value is converted to a string if possible, otherwise, an exception may occur.

Question: Can you reuse a ResultSet object?
Answer: No, once a ResultSet is closed or the statement is executed again, the ResultSet becomes invalid.

Question: How do you retrieve column data by column name in ResultSet?
Answer: Use methods like getString(String columnName) by passing the column name.

2.4 Getting the Results

Question: What does TYPE_SCROLL_SENSITIVE in ResultSet mean?
Answer: It means the ResultSet reflects changes in the database while navigating through the rows.

Question: How do you retrieve auto-generated keys after an INSERT operation?
Answer: Use Statement.RETURN_GENERATED_KEYS and call getGeneratedKeys() on the Statement object.

Question: Can you retrieve binary data from a ResultSet?
Answer: Yes, use the getBytes() or getBlob() methods to retrieve binary data.

Question: What is the purpose of the clearWarnings() method in ResultSet?
Answer: It clears all warnings reported on the current ResultSet.

Question: How do you check if a column is nullable in ResultSet?
Answer: Use the isNullable(int column) method of ResultSetMetaData.

Question: How do you update a column with a null value in ResultSet?
Answer: Use the updateNull(columnIndex) method to set a column to null.

Question: What is the use of the findColumn() method in ResultSet?
Answer: The findColumn(String columnName) method retrieves the column index based on its name.

Question: How do you detect changes in a scroll-sensitive ResultSet?
Answer: Move the cursor to a row and call refreshRow() to reflect database changes.

Question: How do you retrieve the column's precision in a ResultSet?
Answer: Use the getPrecision(int column) method of ResultSetMetaData.

Question: Can you update rows in a ResultSet without committing immediately?
Answer: Yes, changes are buffered until updateRow() is called.

Question: How do you roll back a row update in a ResultSet?
Answer: Use the cancelRowUpdates() method before calling updateRow().

Question: What is the purpose of the getWarnings() method in ResultSet?
Answer: It retrieves the first warning reported on the ResultSet.

Question: How do you retrieve a column's scale in ResultSet?
Answer: Use the getScale(int column) method of ResultSetMetaData.

Question: Can you retrieve rows from a ResultSet based on a condition?
Answer: No, conditions must be specified in the SQL query before retrieving the ResultSet.

Question: What happens if you call getString() on a binary column in ResultSet?
Answer: It converts the binary data to a string, potentially leading to incorrect results.

Question: Can you call close() on a ResultSet twice?
Answer: No, calling close() on a closed ResultSet results in a SQLException.

Question: How do you retrieve the column class name in ResultSet?
Answer: Use the getColumnClassName(int column) method of ResultSetMetaData.

Question: How do you detect if a ResultSet supports updates?
Answer: Check the concurrency level using the getConcurrency() method.

Question: How do you retrieve metadata about the ResultSet itself?
Answer: Use the getMetaData() method to get a ResultSetMetaData object.

Question: What happens if a ResultSet is closed before processing is complete?
Answer: Accessing a closed ResultSet results in a SQLException.

2.5 Updating Database Data

Question: How do you update JSON data in a database column?
Answer: Use PreparedStatement to set JSON strings in the UPDATE query or database-specific JSON functions.

Question: How do you log updates in JDBC for debugging?
Answer: Log the query and parameters before executing the executeUpdate() method.

Question: What is the purpose of the refreshRow() method in updates?
Answer: refreshRow() reloads the current row in an updatable ResultSet from the database to reflect any changes.

Question: How do you update a table with data from a file in JDBC?
Answer: Use a PreparedStatement with data read from the file or a bulk insert/update mechanism like LOAD DATA.
Question: How do you handle concurrent updates in JDBC?
Answer: Use database locks or transaction isolation levels to manage concurrent updates.

Question: How do you update a row based on primary key constraints?
Answer: Use the primary key in the WHERE clause of the UPDATE query.

Question: What happens if an update query violates a database constraint?
Answer: An SQLException is thrown, which should be handled in the application code.

Question: Can you update a column using a correlated subquery?
Answer: Yes, use a correlated subquery in the SET clause to dynamically calculate the column value.

Question: How do you check the affected rows after a batch update?
Answer: The executeBatch() method returns an array of integers indicating the rows affected for each query.

Question: How do you update a specific range of rows in JDBC?
Answer: Use WHERE conditions with range operators, e.g., id BETWEEN 10 AND 20.

Question: How do you rollback an update operation?
Answer: Use the rollback() method on the Connection object to undo changes in the current transaction.

Question: Can you use placeholders for table or column names in PreparedStatement?
Answer: No, placeholders can only be used for values, not for table or column names.

Question: How do you use triggers for update operations?
Answer: Define triggers in the database to automatically perform actions when an update occurs.

Question: How do you update large text data in a database?
Answer: Use the setClob() method of PreparedStatement for large text updates.

Question: How do you update binary data in a database?
Answer: Use the setBlob() method in PreparedStatement to update binary columns.

Question: How do you update a nullable column to a default value?
Answer: Use the default value explicitly in the UPDATE query or check for null before updating.

Question: How do you update a database table using a JOIN?
Answer: Use a JOIN in the UPDATE query to derive values from related tables.

Question: How do you ensure atomicity in a multi-query update?
Answer: Use transactions and commit all updates together or rollback if an error occurs.

Question: How do you handle data type mismatches in updates?
Answer: Ensure proper type conversion in Java and validate data types before updating.

Question: How do you dynamically update columns in JDBC?
Answer: Construct the query string programmatically using the required column names and values.

2.6 Error Checking and the SQLException Class

Question: What is the purpose of the SQLException.getMessage() method?
Answer: It provides a human-readable description of the error.

Question: How do you handle syntax errors in SQL queries?
Answer: Log the query and error message, validate SQL syntax before execution, and fix errors based on the details provided.

Question: How do you handle SQLIntegrityConstraintViolationException?
Answer: Ensure that database constraints like primary keys or foreign keys are not violated during insert or update operations.

Question: What is the use of SQLTimeoutException?
Answer: It indicates that a timeout occurred while waiting for a database operation to complete.

Question: How do you handle failed transactions in JDBC?
Answer: Roll back the transaction using rollback() on the Connection object and log the error.

Question: How do you close JDBC resources in case of an error?
Answer: Use a finally block or try-with-resources to ensure Connection, Statement, and ResultSet are closed properly.

Question: How do you detect duplicate key errors in JDBC?
Answer: Check the error code or SQL state returned in the SQLException for duplicate key violations.

Question: How do you handle driver-specific error codes?
Answer: Map the vendor-specific error codes to user-friendly messages or actions in your application.

Question: What is the SQL state class 08 used for?
Answer: It indicates connection-related errors, such as a lost or failed database connection.

Question: How do you handle insufficient privileges errors in JDBC?
Answer: Log the error, notify the user, and ensure proper privileges are granted to the database user.

Question: How do you detect whether an error is due to data truncation?
Answer: Check the SQL state or error code for data truncation issues during updates or inserts.

Question: How do you use SQLTransientException in error handling?
Answer: Catch SQLTransientException to retry operations that failed due to transient conditions, like deadlocks or network glitches.

Question: How do you log chained SQL exceptions?
Answer: Iterate through all exceptions using getNextException() and log each error.

Question: How do you ensure secure error handling in JDBC?
Answer: Avoid exposing sensitive error details to end users and log detailed errors securely.

Question: How do you detect and handle constraint violations in JDBC?
Answer: Use the SQL state or error code for constraint violations, like 23000 for integrity constraints.

Question: How do you debug invalid column errors in JDBC?
Answer: Verify column names in the SQL query and ensure they match the database schema.

Question: What is the purpose of the BatchUpdateException?
Answer: It indicates an error during batch processing and provides information about successful updates before the error.

Question: How do you recover from a SQLNonTransientConnectionException?
Answer: Re-establish the database connection and retry the failed operation.

Question: How do you validate SQL queries before execution?
Answer: Use a SQL syntax checker or database-specific tools to validate queries.

Question: What are best practices for error handling in JDBC?
Answer: Use structured logging, handle specific exceptions, roll back transactions, and close resources properly.

2.7 The SQLWarning Class

Question: What happens if you call clearWarnings() on a ResultSet?
Answer: It clears all warnings associated with the ResultSet.

Question: How do you check if warnings are cleared successfully?
Answer: After calling clearWarnings(), the getWarnings() method should return null.

Question: Can you retrieve warnings after closing a JDBC object?
Answer: No, warnings cannot be retrieved once the Connection, Statement, or ResultSet is closed.

Question: How do you categorize SQL warnings?
Answer: Use the SQL state or vendor-specific error codes to categorize warnings based on their type.

Question: How do you handle vendor-specific warnings?
Answer: Use the getErrorCode() method to identify and handle vendor-specific warnings appropriately.

Question: Are warnings considered errors in JDBC?
Answer: No, warnings are not errors; they indicate recoverable or non-critical issues.

Question: How do you log multiple warnings efficiently?
Answer: Iterate through the warning chain using getNextWarning() and log each warning with its details.

Question: Can you disable SQL warnings in JDBC?
Answer: No, SQL warnings cannot be disabled but can be ignored or logged without affecting execution.

Question: What is a typical example of an SQL warning?
Answer: A warning may occur when a query results in data truncation or precision loss during an insert or update.

Question: How do you retrieve warnings from a CallableStatement?
Answer: Use the getWarnings() method on the CallableStatement object after executing the stored procedure.

Question: What is the significance of SQL state class 01?
Answer: SQL state class 01 represents warnings, as opposed to errors.

Question: How do you detect warnings for auto-generated keys?
Answer: Retrieve warnings from the Statement or PreparedStatement used to execute the query.

Question: Can warnings occur during transaction operations?
Answer: Yes, warnings may occur during commit or rollback operations if non-critical issues are detected.

Question: How do you identify the source of a warning in JDBC?
Answer: Log the context, such as the object (Connection, Statement, or ResultSet) where the warning occurred.

Question: Can warnings affect performance in JDBC?
Answer: Warnings themselves do not affect performance but handling them improperly (e.g., not clearing) can lead to resource leaks.

Question: What is the recommended practice for handling warnings in production?
Answer: Log warnings for monitoring and troubleshooting, and clear them to maintain clean objects.

Question: How do warnings propagate in chained objects?
Answer: Warnings can propagate across the Connection, Statement, and ResultSet objects if not cleared.

Question: What is the best way to test for warnings in a JDBC application?
Answer: Execute queries or operations that are prone to warnings, like those involving truncation or loss of precision.

Question: How do you integrate SQL warning handling into a monitoring system?
Answer: Capture warnings using getWarnings() and send them to a centralized logging or monitoring system.

Question: Can warnings occur during read-only operations?
Answer: Yes, warnings like data truncation or precision issues can occur even during read-only queries.

2.8 The Statement Interface

Question: How do you retrieve warnings from a Statement?
Answer: Use the getWarnings() method to retrieve any SQL warnings generated during execution.

Question: How do you clear warnings from a Statement?
Answer: Call the clearWarnings() method to clear any warnings associated with the Statement.

Question: How do you cancel an executing query in Statement?
Answer: Use the cancel() method to stop a query that is currently executing.

Question: How do you optimize query execution with Statement?
Answer: Use proper indexing in the database, limit rows fetched using LIMIT, and avoid unnecessary columns in queries.

Question: Can you execute a stored procedure using Statement?
Answer: No, use CallableStatement for executing stored procedures.

Question: How do you retrieve the update count from a Statement?
Answer: Use the getUpdateCount() method to get the number of rows affected by the last DML operation.

Question: What happens if you execute an invalid SQL query using Statement?
Answer: An SQLException is thrown, providing details about the error.

Question: How do you execute dynamic SQL queries with Statement?
Answer: Construct the query string dynamically in your application and pass it to the executeQuery() or executeUpdate() method.

Question: Can you execute parameterized queries with Statement?
Answer: No, use PreparedStatement for parameterized queries.

Question: How do you handle large result sets in Statement?
Answer: Use the setFetchSize(int rows) method to control the number of rows fetched at a time.

Question: What is the default fetch size for a Statement?
Answer: The default fetch size depends on the database and JDBC driver.

Question: How do you retrieve multiple result sets from a query?
Answer: Use the execute() method and then call getMoreResults() to iterate through the result sets.

Question: How do you clear a batch of SQL queries in Statement?
Answer: Use the clearBatch() method to remove all queries from the batch.

Question: Can you retrieve metadata using a Statement?
Answer: Yes, execute a query and use the ResultSet.getMetaData() method to retrieve column metadata.

Question: How do you execute DCL queries (e.g., GRANT, REVOKE) using Statement?
Answer: Use the executeUpdate() method to execute DCL queries.

Question: How do you handle long-running queries in Statement?
Answer: Set a query timeout using setQueryTimeout() or execute queries asynchronously if supported by the driver.

Question: Can you cache queries with Statement?
Answer: No, Statement does not provide query caching; use a caching layer or database-specific features.

Question: How do you execute a query and retrieve generated keys?
Answer: Use the executeUpdate(String sql, int autoGeneratedKeys) method and call getGeneratedKeys().

Question: Can you execute a transaction with Statement?
Answer: Yes, use setAutoCommit(false) on the Connection, execute statements, and commit or rollback the transaction.

Question: What are the limitations of using Statement in JDBC?
Answer: Statement lacks support for parameterized queries, is vulnerable to SQL injection, and is less efficient compared to PreparedStatement.

2.9 PreparedStatement

Question: How do you use PreparedStatement for batch updates?
Answer: Set parameters for each query, use addBatch() to add them to the batch, and call executeBatch() to execute.

Question: What are the performance benefits of using PreparedStatement?
Answer: It precompiles SQL queries, reducing parsing overhead, and is efficient for repeated executions.

Question: How do you retrieve warnings from a PreparedStatement?
Answer: Use the getWarnings() method to retrieve SQL warnings related to the query.

Question: Can you use PreparedStatement for dynamic table or column names?
Answer: No, table and column names cannot be parameterized. Use string concatenation cautiously for such cases.

Question: How do you debug a PreparedStatement?
Answer: Log the SQL query string and parameter values before execution for troubleshooting.

Question: Can a PreparedStatement handle multiple result sets?
Answer: No, use CallableStatement for handling multiple result sets.

Question: How do you optimize query execution with PreparedStatement?
Answer: Use connection pooling, parameterized queries, and efficient indexing in the database.

Question: How do you handle NULL values in PreparedStatement?
Answer: Use the setNull() method with the appropriate SQL type for the parameter.

Question: Can you use a PreparedStatement for DDL operations?
Answer: No, PreparedStatement is primarily used for DML and SELECT queries.

Question: How do you set a timestamp in a PreparedStatement?
Answer: Use the setTimestamp(int parameterIndex, Timestamp value) method.

Question: What happens if you don't set all placeholders in a PreparedStatement?
Answer: An SQLException is thrown indicating incomplete parameter binding.

Question: How do you handle exceptions during batch processing in PreparedStatement?
Answer: Catch BatchUpdateException and check getUpdateCounts() for the status of each query in the batch.

Question: How do you close a PreparedStatement in JDBC?
Answer: Use the close() method to release resources associated with the PreparedStatement.

Question: Can you execute multiple queries with a single PreparedStatement?
Answer: No, each PreparedStatement is tied to a specific SQL query.

Question: How do you handle a timeout in a PreparedStatement?
Answer: Use the setQueryTimeout(int seconds) method to set a timeout for query execution.

Question: How do you update multiple rows using a PreparedStatement?
Answer: Set parameters for each row and use batch processing to execute updates.

Question: How do you handle exceptions when executing a PreparedStatement?
Answer: Use a try-catch block to catch SQLException and log the error details.

Question: What are the limitations of PreparedStatement?
Answer: It cannot handle dynamic table/column names or execute stored procedures.

Question: How do you manage connections for a PreparedStatement in a web application?
Answer: Use a connection pool to manage connections efficiently in high-traffic applications.

Question: How do you ensure secure and efficient database interaction with PreparedStatement?
Answer: Use connection pooling, parameterized queries, and close resources in a finally block or with try-with-resources.

2.10 CallableStatement

Question: How do you handle database-specific data types in CallableStatement?
Answer: Use database-specific SQL types or custom data types as defined in the JDBC driver documentation.

Question: How do you optimize stored procedure execution in JDBC?
Answer: Use connection pooling, reuse CallableStatement objects, and ensure proper indexing in the database.

Question: How do you log CallableStatement execution for debugging?
Answer: Log the SQL call string and parameter values before executing the CallableStatement.

Question: Can CallableStatement handle large objects like BLOBs or CLOBs?
Answer: Yes, use setBlob() or setClob() to bind large objects to input parameters.

Question: How do you handle output parameters that return arrays?
Answer: Use getArray() to retrieve an array from an output parameter.

Question: What happens if you don't register an output parameter in CallableStatement?
Answer: An SQLException is thrown when you attempt to retrieve the unregistered output parameter.

Question: Can you use CallableStatement for dynamic table or column names?
Answer: No, CallableStatement does not support dynamic table or column names directly.

Question: How do you ensure thread safety with CallableStatement?
Answer: Use a separate CallableStatement object for each thread or synchronize access to shared objects.

Question: How do you retrieve metadata for a CallableStatement?
Answer: Use the ParameterMetaData object obtained with the getParameterMetaData() method.

Question: How do you handle batch execution errors in CallableStatement?
Answer: Catch BatchUpdateException and analyze the getUpdateCounts() array for error details.

Question: How do you debug issues with stored procedures in CallableStatement?
Answer: Log the procedure call, parameter values, and database responses for troubleshooting.

Question: What is the purpose of clearParameters() in CallableStatement?
Answer: The clearParameters() method resets all input and output parameters for reuse.

Question: How do you handle stored procedures with variable numbers of parameters?
Answer: Use conditional logic in your code to dynamically construct the CallableStatement and bind parameters.

Question: Can you execute a stored procedure asynchronously in JDBC?
Answer: No, JDBC does not natively support asynchronous execution; use application-level threading for parallelism.

Question: How do you retrieve the SQL state from a CallableStatement exception?
Answer: Use the getSQLState() method of the SQLException object.

Question: How do you call a stored procedure with a return type in JDBC?
Answer: Use {? = call procedureName(?)} syntax, register the return type, and retrieve it with a getter method.

Question: What is the difference between CallableStatement and Statement?
Answer: CallableStatement executes stored procedures, while Statement executes static SQL queries.

Question: How do you execute a procedure that modifies multiple tables?
Answer: Call the procedure with CallableStatement and handle any transactional logic in the database.

Question: Can you use CallableStatement with database functions returning complex types?
Answer: Yes, register the output as a ResultSet or custom type, depending on database support.

Question: How do you ensure secure stored procedure execution in JDBC?
Answer: Use parameterized queries with CallableStatement, implement least privilege, and validate input data.

2.11 The ResultSet Interface

Question: What is the difference between TYPE_SCROLL_SENSITIVE and TYPE_SCROLL_INSENSITIVE?
Answer: TYPE_SCROLL_SENSITIVE reflects database changes, while TYPE_SCROLL_INSENSITIVE does not.

Question: Can you update data in a ResultSet?
Answer: Yes, use an updatable ResultSet and methods like updateString() and updateRow().

Question: How do you delete a row in an updatable ResultSet?
Answer: Use the deleteRow() method to remove the current row.

Question: How do you insert a new row into a ResultSet?
Answer: Use moveToInsertRow(), set column values, and call insertRow().

Question: What does the refreshRow() method do in ResultSet?
Answer: It reloads the current row's data from the database, reflecting any updates made.

Question: How do you navigate backward in a ResultSet?
Answer: Use the previous() method in a scrollable ResultSet.

Question: What is the purpose of getConcurrency() in ResultSet?
Answer: It returns the concurrency mode (CONCUR_READ_ONLY or CONCUR_UPDATABLE) of the ResultSet.

Question: How do you close a ResultSet?
Answer: Call the close() method to release resources associated with the ResultSet.

Question: What is the significance of the beforeFirst() method in ResultSet?
Answer: It positions the cursor before the first row of the ResultSet.

Question: How do you navigate to a relative row in a ResultSet?
Answer: Use the relative(int rows) method to move the cursor relative to its current position.

Question: Can a ResultSet contain multiple result sets?
Answer: No, a ResultSet represents a single set of query results; use Statement for multiple result sets.

Question: What happens if you try to retrieve data after closing a ResultSet?
Answer: An SQLException is thrown, indicating that the ResultSet is closed.

Question: How do you retrieve warnings from a ResultSet?
Answer: Use the getWarnings() method to fetch warnings related to the query results.

Question: How do you retrieve the current row number in a ResultSet?
Answer: Use the getRow() method to get the current row's position.

Question: What does the afterLast() method do in a ResultSet?
Answer: It moves the cursor to a position after the last row.

Question: How do you retrieve column names from a ResultSet?
Answer: Use the getColumnName(int columnIndex) method of ResultSetMetaData.

Question: Can you reuse a ResultSet after it is closed?
Answer: No, a closed ResultSet cannot be reused.

Question: How do you handle large result sets efficiently in ResultSet?
Answer: Use setFetchSize() to control the number of rows fetched at a time.

Question: How do you update a column to null in a ResultSet?
Answer: Use the updateNull(int columnIndex) method.

Question: What is the purpose of findColumn() in ResultSet?
Answer: It retrieves the index of a column based on its name.

2.12 Updatable Result Sets

Question: What happens if you call deleteRow() twice on the same row?
Answer: An SQLException is thrown, indicating that the row is no longer valid for deletion.

Question: Can you update computed columns in an updatable ResultSet?
Answer: No, computed columns cannot be updated; only actual table columns can be modified.

Question: How do you update multiple columns in an updatable ResultSet?
Answer: Call updateXXX() for each column and then call updateRow() to save all changes together.

Question: What is the role of ResultSetMetaData in an updatable ResultSet?
Answer: ResultSetMetaData provides information about the columns, such as their types and names, which can be used for dynamic updates.

Question: Can you use batch updates with an updatable ResultSet?
Answer: No, batch updates are handled separately using Statement or PreparedStatement.

Question: How do you navigate rows in an updatable ResultSet?
Answer: Use methods like next(), previous(), first(), last(), absolute(), and relative().

Question: How do you handle exceptions in an updatable ResultSet?
Answer: Use a try-catch block to catch SQLException and ensure proper resource management.

Question: Can you update rows using a JOIN query in an updatable ResultSet?
Answer: No, the query must select from a single table to be updatable.

Question: How do you retrieve the number of rows updated by updateRow()?
Answer: Use the getUpdateCount() method on the associated Statement object.

Question: What happens if you try to update a non-updatable column?
Answer: An SQLException is thrown indicating that the column cannot be updated.

Question: Can you update rows in a ResultSet that uses a view?
Answer: Only if the view is updatable and meets the database's criteria for updates.

Question: How do you handle large data updates in an updatable ResultSet?
Answer: Use updateClob() or updateBlob() methods for large text or binary data.

Question: How do you manage transactions with an updatable ResultSet?
Answer: Disable auto-commit using setAutoCommit(false) and use commit() or rollback() after updates.

Question: Can you insert rows into a table with default values in an updatable ResultSet?
Answer: Yes, skip setting the columns with default values; they will be automatically populated by the database.

Question: How do you ensure consistency between the ResultSet and the database?
Answer: Use refreshRow() to reload the current row from the database after any external changes.

Question: What is the significance of getConcurrency() in an updatable ResultSet?
Answer: It ensures that the ResultSet is created with CONCUR_UPDATABLE mode for updates.

Question: Can you use aggregate functions in an updatable ResultSet?
Answer: No, queries with aggregate functions are not updatable.

Question: How do you revert changes in an updatable ResultSet?
Answer: Use the cancelRowUpdates() method before calling updateRow().

Question: How do you update rows conditionally in an updatable ResultSet?
Answer: Navigate to the desired row, check conditions programmatically, and use updateXXX() methods.

Question: What are the best practices for using updatable ResultSet?
Answer: Use simple queries, manage transactions carefully, and close resources to avoid memory leaks.

2.13 JDBC Types

Question: What is the JDBC type for SQL REAL?
Answer: SQL REAL maps to the Java float class.

Question: How do you handle SQL TIME in JDBC?
Answer: SQL TIME maps to java.sql.Time in Java.

Question: How do you retrieve a SQL STRUCT type in JDBC?
Answer: SQL STRUCT maps to java.sql.Struct, and getStruct() is used to retrieve it.

Question: Can you use custom data types in JDBC?
Answer: Yes, SQL user-defined types can be mapped using java.sql.SQLData and custom implementations.

Question: What is the JDBC type for SQL LONGVARCHAR?
Answer: SQL LONGVARCHAR maps to the Java String class, used for long text data.

Question: How does JDBC handle SQL NVARCHAR?
Answer: SQL NVARCHAR maps to the Java String class, supporting Unicode data.

Question: What is the Java equivalent for SQL VARBINARY?
Answer: SQL VARBINARY maps to the Java byte[] array.

Question: How do you handle SQL XML data in JDBC?
Answer: SQL XML maps to java.sql.SQLXML, and methods like getSQLXML() and setSQLXML() are used.

Question: What is the JDBC type for SQL ROWID?
Answer: SQL ROWID maps to java.sql.RowId.

Question: How do you handle SQL REF types in JDBC?
Answer: SQL REF maps to java.sql.Ref, and getRef() and setRef() are used for retrieval and binding.

Question: How does JDBC handle SQL LONGVARBINARY?
Answer: SQL LONGVARBINARY maps to the Java byte[] array for handling large binary data.

Question: Can you retrieve custom database objects using JDBC types?
Answer: Yes, use SQL types like STRUCT and map them to Java classes using SQLData.

Question: What is the difference between SQL TEXT and CLOB in JDBC?
Answer: Both are used for large text data, but TEXT maps to String, while CLOB maps to java.sql.Clob.

Question: How do you handle SQL NCHAR in JDBC?
Answer: SQL NCHAR maps to the Java String class, supporting fixed-length Unicode data.

Question: How do you map SQL ENUM to a Java type?
Answer: SQL ENUM can be mapped to a Java String or Enum using application logic.

Question: What is the JDBC type for SQL GEOMETRY?
Answer: SQL GEOMETRY is database-specific and typically mapped to custom Java classes or byte[].

Question: How do you handle SQL JSON data in JDBC?
Answer: SQL JSON can be mapped to a String or a custom parser to convert it into Java objects.

Question: What is the purpose of JDBC type mappings?
Answer: JDBC type mappings ensure seamless data transfer between Java applications and relational databases.

Question: How do you retrieve the database type of a column in a ResultSet?
Answer: Use the getColumnType(int columnIndex) method from ResultSetMetaData.

Question: How do you bind SQL types dynamically in JDBC?
Answer: Use the setObject() method, specifying the object and the SQL type dynamically.

2.14 Executing SQL Queries

Question: How do you use PreparedStatement for executing queries?
Answer: Use PreparedStatement for parameterized queries by setting values using setter methods and executing with executeQuery() or executeUpdate().

Question: How do you cancel a running query in JDBC?
Answer: Use the cancel() method of the Statement object to cancel an executing query.

Question: How do you execute a SELECT query in JDBC?
Answer: Use the executeQuery() method, which returns a ResultSet containing the query results.

Question: How do you handle SQL injection while executing queries?
Answer: Use PreparedStatement instead of directly concatenating user input into SQL queries.

Question: Can you execute SQL queries asynchronously in JDBC?
Answer: JDBC does not natively support asynchronous execution; you can use application-level threading for parallel execution.

Question: How do you retrieve the execution time of a query?
Answer: Measure the time using System.currentTimeMillis() before and after query execution.

Question: How do you execute a SQL query with complex joins?
Answer: Construct the query with necessary joins and execute it using Statement or PreparedStatement.

Question: How do you pass null values in a SQL query?
Answer: Use the setNull(int parameterIndex, int sqlType) method in PreparedStatement.

Question: Can you use JDBC to execute queries on multiple databases?
Answer: Yes, establish separate Connection objects for each database and execute queries independently.

Question: How do you optimize query execution in JDBC?
Answer: Use indexed columns, proper fetch sizes, connection pooling, and parameterized queries to optimize execution.

Question: What is the role of Statement.closeOnCompletion()?
Answer: It ensures the Statement object is automatically closed when the associated ResultSet is closed.

Question: How do you execute an update with conditional logic?
Answer: Construct the SQL query with WHERE clauses and execute it using executeUpdate().

Question: How do you execute a SQL query that returns metadata?
Answer: Execute the query and use ResultSetMetaData from the returned ResultSet.

Question: Can you execute queries with custom database functions?
Answer: Yes, include the custom function in the query and execute it like a regular SQL statement.

Question: How do you handle failed batch executions?
Answer: Catch BatchUpdateException and analyze the getUpdateCounts() array for execution details.

Question: What is the difference between executeQuery() and execute() for SELECT?
Answer: executeQuery() directly returns a ResultSet, while execute() requires calling getResultSet() to retrieve it.

Question: How do you ensure a query's result is processed in order?
Answer: JDBC processes query results in the order rows are returned by the database.

Question: How do you test a query before executing it in JDBC?
Answer: Log or print the constructed query string for validation before execution.

Question: How do you retrieve large binary data from a query?
Answer: Use getBlob() or getBytes() methods from the ResultSet.

Question: What are the best practices for executing queries in JDBC?
Answer: Use parameterized queries, proper exception handling, and close resources using try-with-resources.

2.15 ResultSetMetaData

Question: How do you get the catalog name of a column?
Answer: Use the getCatalogName(int columnIndex) method to retrieve the catalog name.

Question: What is the use of getColumnTypeName(int columnIndex) in ResultSetMetaData?
Answer: It returns the database-specific type name of the column, such as VARCHAR or INTEGER.

Question: Can ResultSetMetaData provide default values for columns?
Answer: No, ResultSetMetaData does not provide default values; such details can be retrieved from DatabaseMetaData.

Question: How do you check the nullability of a column?
Answer: Use the isNullable(int columnIndex) method to check if a column can contain null values.

Question: How do you iterate over all columns in a ResultSet?
Answer: Use a loop with getColumnCount() and retrieve metadata for each column using methods like getColumnName() or getColumnType().

Question: Can you retrieve metadata for a computed column?
Answer: Yes, ResultSetMetaData provides metadata for computed columns, such as their type and name.

Question: How do you determine if a column is searchable?
Answer: Use the isSearchable(int columnIndex) method to check if a column can be used in a WHERE clause.

Question: How do you retrieve metadata for columns in a view?
Answer: Execute a SELECT query on the view and use ResultSetMetaData for the returned columns.

Question: How do you handle exceptions when using ResultSetMetaData?
Answer: Use a try-catch block to catch SQLException during metadata retrieval.

Question: Can you use ResultSetMetaData to modify table schemas?
Answer: No, ResultSetMetaData is read-only and cannot modify database schemas.

Question: How do you determine if a column is case-sensitive?
Answer: Use the isCaseSensitive(int columnIndex) method to check if a column's data is case-sensitive.

Question: Can you retrieve the default value of a column using ResultSetMetaData?
Answer: No, ResultSetMetaData does not provide default values for columns.

Question: How do you retrieve information about an alias column?
Answer: Use getColumnLabel(int columnIndex) to get the alias name, if defined.

Question: How do you retrieve metadata for a query involving joins?
Answer: Execute the query and use ResultSetMetaData to retrieve column information for all columns in the result set.

Question: Can you use ResultSetMetaData for dynamic queries?
Answer: Yes, ResultSetMetaData is often used to dynamically retrieve and process column information for dynamic queries.

Question: How do you ensure the column index is valid in ResultSetMetaData?
Answer: Validate against the value returned by getColumnCount() to avoid SQLException.

Question: How do you use ResultSetMetaData in a reporting application?
Answer: Use it to dynamically retrieve column names, types, and other details for building reports.

Question: Can ResultSetMetaData detect column constraints?
Answer: No, use DatabaseMetaData for column constraints like primary keys or foreign keys.

Question: How do you handle performance issues with ResultSetMetaData?
Answer: Use it sparingly and cache metadata if needed, especially for frequently executed queries.

Question: What are the best practices for using ResultSetMetaData?
Answer: Use it for dynamic column processing, validate column indexes, and close ResultSet objects after use.

2.16 Executing SQL Updates

Question: How do you handle exceptions during updates?
Answer: Use a try-catch block to catch SQLException and log or handle the exception.

Question: How do you update multiple rows in a single query?
Answer: Use SQL statements with conditions like WHERE or perform bulk updates using batch processing.

Question: Can you execute a stored procedure for updates?
Answer: Yes, use CallableStatement to execute stored procedures for update operations.

Question: How do you test update queries in JDBC?
Answer: Execute the query in a test environment and verify the changes in the database.

Question: Can you execute an update query using ResultSet?
Answer: Yes, use an updatable ResultSet with methods like updateRow() or deleteRow().

Question: How do you handle constraints during updates?
Answer: Ensure the update query adheres to database constraints like primary keys or foreign keys.

Question: Can you update columns with computed values in JDBC?
Answer: Yes, include computed values in the SQL query using expressions like SET column = value * 2.

Question: How do you execute a conditional update based on another table?
Answer: Use subqueries or JOIN clauses in the SQL update statement.

Question: How do you handle large-scale updates efficiently?
Answer: Use batch processing, partitioned updates, and proper indexing for large-scale updates.

Question: What is the purpose of clearBatch() in batch updates?
Answer: The clearBatch() method removes all SQL commands added to the batch.

Question: How do you update a column to null in JDBC?
Answer: Use the setNull() method in PreparedStatement or SQL syntax like SET column = NULL.

Question: Can you execute an update with nested transactions?
Answer: JDBC does not natively support nested transactions, but you can manage them programmatically.

Question: How do you retrieve the auto-generated ID after an update?
Answer: Use Statement.RETURN_GENERATED_KEYS and call getGeneratedKeys().

Question: How do you update multiple tables in one query?
Answer: Use SQL statements with JOIN clauses or execute multiple update queries in a batch.

Question: How do you prevent deadlocks during updates?
Answer: Use proper indexing, avoid long-running transactions, and execute updates in a consistent order.

Question: Can you update rows in a view using JDBC?
Answer: Yes, but only if the view is updatable as per the database's configuration.

Question: How do you handle update conflicts in concurrent environments?
Answer: Use locking mechanisms or optimistic concurrency control by checking version numbers.

Question: How do you rollback updates in batch processing?
Answer: Use setAutoCommit(false) and call rollback() if an exception occurs during executeBatch().

Question: How do you update JSON data in a database using JDBC?
Answer: Use SQL queries with JSON manipulation functions supported by the database.

Question: What are the best practices for executing updates in JDBC?
Answer: Use parameterized queries, enable transactions, log queries, and optimize SQL statements for performance.

2.17 Transaction Management

Question: Can you perform nested transactions in JDBC?
Answer: JDBC does not natively support nested transactions, but savepoints can mimic similar functionality

Question: What is a distributed transaction?
Answer: A distributed transaction spans multiple databases or resource managers and ensures consistency across them.

Question: How do you manage distributed transactions in Java?
Answer: Use Java Transaction API (JTA) or frameworks like Hibernate for managing distributed transactions.

Question: How do you detect deadlocks in transactions?
Answer: Use database monitoring tools or query logs to identify and resolve deadlocks.

Question: What is the difference between rollback and rollback to savepoint?
Answer: rollback() undoes all changes in the transaction, while rollback(Savepoint savepoint) undoes changes only up to the specified savepoint.

Question: Can you use transactions in read-only operations?
Answer: Yes, transactions can group read-only operations for consistency but do not require commit or rollback.

Question: How do you handle long-running transactions?
Answer: Break them into smaller units or use savepoints to manage intermediate states.

Question: How do you test transaction behavior?
Answer: Use unit tests with mock databases or test environments to simulate transaction scenarios.

Question: How do you log transaction activities in JDBC?
Answer: Log each step of the transaction, including commits, rollbacks, and exceptions.

Question: Can you perform transactions across different JDBC drivers?
Answer: Yes, but you need a transaction manager like JTA to coordinate transactions across multiple drivers.

Question: How do you set a transaction timeout in JDBC?
Answer: JDBC does not directly support transaction timeouts; manage timeouts at the application or database level.

Question: Can you use multiple savepoints in a transaction?
Answer: Yes, multiple savepoints can be created, and you can roll back to any of them as needed.

Question: How do you optimize transaction performance?
Answer: Use indexing, reduce the transaction scope, and avoid locking unnecessary resources.

Question: What are phantom reads in transactions?
Answer: Phantom reads occur when new rows are added by other transactions and affect the results of a repeated query.

Question: How do you avoid phantom reads in JDBC?
Answer: Use the TRANSACTION_SERIALIZABLE isolation level to prevent phantom reads.

Question: What are dirty reads in transactions?
Answer: Dirty reads occur when a transaction reads uncommitted changes from another transaction.

Question: How do you prevent dirty reads in JDBC?
Answer: Use the TRANSACTION_READ_COMMITTED isolation level to prevent dirty reads.

Question: Can you commit a transaction after rolling back?
Answer: No, after a rollback, the transaction is effectively ended, and you must start a new transaction.

Question: What is the two-phase commit protocol?
Answer: The two-phase commit protocol ensures atomicity across distributed transactions by involving a prepare and commit phase.

Question: What are best practices for transaction management in JDBC?
Answer: Use proper transaction boundaries, log activities, handle exceptions gracefully, and optimize for performance.

Online Resources

	Practice Paper	YouTube Video Playlist Link
Link	https://forms.gle/DbWhhgW6MczMDuw99	https://www.youtube.com/playlist?list=PLzlh_31VWEFpAiZLj3UJPkHzZrDjgBcgE
QR Code		

CHAPTER 3
Introduction to Java EE

3.1 Overview of Java EE

Question: What is the difference between Stateless and Stateful EJBs?
Answer: Stateless EJBs do not maintain client state, while Stateful EJBs maintain conversational state for a client.

Question: What is the use of the Timer Service in Java EE?
Answer: The Timer Service allows scheduling tasks like sending notifications or batch processing in enterprise applications.

Question: How does Java EE ensure portability across application servers?
Answer: Java EE follows standard specifications, ensuring applications can run on any compliant application server.

Question: What is the purpose of JPA in Java EE?
Answer: JPA (Java Persistence API) simplifies database interaction by providing an object-relational mapping framework.

Question: What is the role of the Interceptor API in Java EE?
Answer: The Interceptor API enables cross-cutting concerns like logging and auditing to be applied to business methods.

Question: What is the purpose of the Batch API in Java EE?
Answer: The Batch API is used for processing large volumes of data in batch jobs.

Question: How does Java EE handle internationalization?
Answer: Java EE supports internationalization using resource bundles and localization features.

Question: What is the purpose of the Connector API in Java EE?
Answer: The Connector API integrates Java EE applications with legacy systems or external enterprise systems.

Question: What is the difference between Servlet 2.5 and Servlet 3.0 in Java EE?
Answer: Servlet 3.0 introduced features like annotations, asynchronous processing, and pluggability.

Question: What is the purpose of Managed Beans in Java EE?
Answer: Managed Beans provide lightweight dependency injection and act as a central point for managing application logic.

Question: How does Java EE handle session management?
Answer: Java EE manages sessions using HTTP sessions, Stateful EJBs, or custom implementations.

Question: What is a Java EE Profile?
Answer: A Java EE profile defines a subset of the full Java EE platform for specific application requirements, such as the Web Profile.

Question: What is a Java EE Web Profile?
Answer: The Web Profile is a lightweight subset of Java EE for developing web applications.

Question: How does Java EE handle scalability?
Answer: Java EE handles scalability through features like load balancing, clustering, and resource pooling.

Question: How do you deploy a Java EE application?

Answer: Package the application into WAR or EAR files and deploy them on a Java EE-compliant application server.

Question: What is the purpose of annotations in Java EE?
Answer: Annotations simplify configuration by replacing XML descriptors for components like Servlets and EJBs.

Question: How does Java EE support RESTful web services?
Answer: Java EE uses the JAX-RS API to create and consume RESTful web services.

Question: How does Java EE ensure backward compatibility?
Answer: Java EE maintains backward compatibility by adhering to consistent API specifications.

Question: What are the advantages of using Java EE for enterprise applications?
Answer: Java EE provides portability, scalability, security, and a wide range of APIs for enterprise development.

Question: What is the future of Java EE after Jakarta EE?
Answer: Java EE has transitioned to Jakarta EE, focusing on cloud-native and modern enterprise application development.

3.2 Features and Benefits of Java EE

Question: How does Java EE handle cross-cutting concerns?
Answer: Java EE handles cross-cutting concerns like logging, security, and transactions using Interceptors and declarative configurations.

Question: How does Java EE ensure reliability?
Answer: Java EE ensures reliability with robust error handling, exception management, and transaction rollback features.

Question: What is the significance of the Connector API in Java EE?
Answer: The Connector API integrates Java EE applications with external or legacy systems.

Question: How does Java EE support asynchronous operations?
Answer: Java EE supports asynchronous operations with JMS and asynchronous Servlets.

Question: What is the role of Managed Beans in Java EE?
Answer: Managed Beans provide a lightweight and versatile component model for business logic.

Question: How does Java EE promote code reuse?
Answer: Java EE promotes code reuse with components like EJBs and common utility APIs.

Question: How does Java EE ensure backward compatibility?
Answer: Java EE maintains backward compatibility by adhering to consistent API specifications and standards.

Question: How does Java EE handle batch processing?
Answer: Java EE provides a Batch API for processing large volumes of data efficiently.

Question: How does Java EE manage resources?
Answer: Java EE manages resources like database connections, threads, and JMS connections using resource pooling.

Question: What is the advantage of the JPA API in Java EE?
Answer: JPA simplifies database interaction by automating object-relational mapping.

Question: How does Java EE enable rapid development?

Answer: Java EE enables rapid development with pre-defined standards, reusable components, and integrated tools.

Question: What is the advantage of standardized APIs in Java EE?
Answer: Standardized APIs ensure interoperability and portability across different application servers.

Question: How does Java EE support cloud-based deployments?
Answer: Java EE supports cloud-based deployments with lightweight profiles and scalability features.

Question: How does Java EE ensure security during deployment?
Answer: Java EE ensures security with role-based access control, encrypted communication, and secure configurations.

Question: What is the advantage of application server clustering in Java EE?
Answer: Clustering enhances fault tolerance and load balancing for Java EE applications.

Question: How does Java EE facilitate third-party integration?
Answer: Java EE facilitates integration with third-party tools and services using standard APIs like JCA and JNDI.

Question: How does Java EE promote application maintainability?
Answer: Java EE promotes maintainability through modular components, standard practices, and clear separation of concerns.

Question: How does Java EE support microservices?
Answer: Java EE supports microservices with lightweight containers and APIs like JAX-RS for RESTful communication.

Question: What is the significance of the Bean Validation API?
Answer: The Bean Validation API ensures data integrity by enforcing validation rules on bean properties.

Question: What are the key benefits of using Java EE?
Answer: Key benefits include portability, scalability, security, rapid development, and a robust ecosystem of tools and libraries.

3.3 Evolution of Java EE

Question: How did JPA impact Java EE?
Answer: JPA replaced complex EJB entity beans with a simpler, standardized object-relational mapping framework.

Question: What role did the Java Community Process (JCP) play in Java EE?
Answer: The JCP guided the development and standardization of Java EE through community-driven specifications.

Question: How did Java EE support web services evolution?
Answer: Java EE introduced APIs like JAX-RPC and JAX-WS for SOAP-based services and JAX-RS for RESTful services.

Question: How did Java EE adopt microservices architecture?
Answer: Java EE adopted microservices with Jakarta EE, introducing lightweight APIs and cloud-native features.

Question: What is the role of CDI in modern Java EE?
Answer: CDI provided a unified dependency injection model, enhancing modularity and reducing boilerplate code.

Question: How did Java EE embrace cloud-native development?
Answer: Java EE 8 and Jakarta EE included features like container orchestration support and lightweight deployment models.

Question: How did annotations transform Java EE development?
Answer: Annotations reduced reliance on XML configuration, simplifying the development and deployment process.

Question: How did Java EE adapt to HTTP/2?
Answer: Java EE 8 introduced Servlet 4.0 with native HTTP/2 support for improved web application performance.

Question: How did Java EE influence modern frameworks?
Answer: Java EE set standards for APIs and architectures, influencing frameworks like Spring and Micronaut.

Question: How has Jakarta EE addressed innovation challenges?
Answer: Jakarta EE introduced open-source contributions and faster release cycles to foster innovation.

Question: What is the significance of modularization in Java EE?
Answer: Modularization allowed Java EE to support lightweight profiles and reduce resource overhead.

Question: How did the Batch API enhance Java EE?
Answer: The Batch API provided efficient mechanisms for processing large data sets in enterprise applications.

Question: What led to the creation of the Web Profile?
Answer: The Web Profile was introduced to address the needs of web developers requiring a lighter subset of Java EE.

Question: How does Jakarta EE plan for the future?
Answer: Jakarta EE focuses on cloud-native architectures, modern tools, and community-driven innovation.

Question: What is the impact of Java EE's backward compatibility?
Answer: Backward compatibility ensured seamless migration for legacy applications, preserving investment in enterprise solutions.

Question: How did Java EE evolve to support modern security needs?
Answer: Java EE introduced enhanced security APIs, such as OAuth and JWT support, for modern enterprise applications.

Question: How does Jakarta EE integrate with Kubernetes?
Answer: Jakarta EE supports containerization and orchestration tools like Kubernetes, enabling scalable deployments.

Question: How did Java EE address developer community concerns?
Answer: Java EE reduced complexity, enhanced developer productivity, and increased transparency through community feedback.

Question: What role do microservices play in Jakarta EE's roadmap?
Answer: Jakarta EE emphasizes microservices, enabling developers to build modular and lightweight applications.

Question: Why is the evolution of Java EE significant?
Answer: The evolution of Java EE demonstrates its adaptability to changing technologies, ensuring relevance in modern enterprise development.

3.4 Java EE Architecture and Components

Question: How does Java EE handle SOAP-based web services?
Answer: Java EE uses JAX-WS for creating and consuming SOAP-based web services.

Question: What is the role of the Connector API in Java EE?
Answer: The Connector API integrates Java EE applications with external or legacy enterprise systems.

Question: What is the role of the Bean Validation API in Java EE?
Answer: The Bean Validation API enforces constraints on bean properties, ensuring data integrity.

Question: What is the role of Interceptors in Java EE?
Answer: Interceptors handle cross-cutting concerns like logging, auditing, and transaction management.

Question: How does Java EE handle asynchronous operations?
Answer: Java EE handles asynchronous operations with JMS, asynchronous Servlets, and EJB timers.

Question: How does Java EE support internationalization?
Answer: Java EE uses resource bundles and locale-specific configurations to support internationalization.

Question: What is the purpose of CDI in Java EE?
Answer: CDI (Contexts and Dependency Injection) manages dependencies and provides lifecycle management for Java EE components.

Question: What is the purpose of the Batch API in Java EE?
Answer: The Batch API processes large data sets efficiently in batch jobs.

Question: How does Java EE manage resources like connections?
Answer: Java EE uses resource pooling to manage database connections, JMS sessions, and other resources.

Question: What is the importance of modular architecture in Java EE?
Answer: Modular architecture ensures scalability, reusability, and maintainability of enterprise applications.

Question: What is the Web Profile in Java EE?
Answer: The Web Profile is a subset of Java EE, optimized for web applications.

Question: How does Java EE integrate with databases?
Answer: Java EE integrates with databases using JPA and JDBC for efficient data persistence and management.

Question: How does Java EE handle exceptions?
Answer: Java EE provides exception handling through standard APIs and declarative configurations in deployment descriptors.

Question: What is the advantage of using EJBs in the business tier?
Answer: EJBs simplify business logic with built-in support for transactions, security, and concurrency.

Question: How does Java EE support microservices?
Answer: Java EE supports microservices with lightweight APIs like JAX-RS and containerized deployment models.

Question: How does Java EE ensure application portability?
Answer: Java EE applications are portable across compliant servers due to adherence to standard specifications.

Question: What is the role of resource adapters in Java EE?
Answer: Resource adapters connect Java EE applications to external systems or legacy platforms.

Question: How does Java EE handle cloud-based applications?
Answer: Java EE supports cloud applications with container orchestration and lightweight deployment options.

Question: How does Java EE enable scalability?
Answer: Java EE ensures scalability through clustering, load balancing, and distributed resource management.

Question: What are the key benefits of Java EE architecture?
Answer: Key benefits include modular design, portability, scalability, robust security, and support for enterprise-grade applications.

3.5 Java EE Development and Deployment

Question: How does Java EE handle scalability during deployment?
Answer: Java EE handles scalability with clustering, load balancing, and resource pooling at the server level.

Question: What is the role of context roots in Java EE applications?
Answer: The context root defines the URL prefix used to access the application.

Question: How do you monitor Java EE applications after deployment?
Answer: Use tools like server admin consoles, logging frameworks, and monitoring tools (e.g., JMX, New Relic).

Question: How does Java EE handle session management in web applications?
Answer: Java EE uses HTTP sessions, cookies, and URL rewriting for session management.

Question: What is the purpose of the application.xml file in EAR deployment?
Answer: The application.xml file defines the structure and module configuration for an EAR package.

Question: How do you secure Java EE applications during deployment?
Answer: Configure HTTPS, role-based access control, and secure JNDI resources in the deployment settings.

Question: What is the role of CDI during deployment?
Answer: CDI manages dependencies and context lifecycle for Java EE components at runtime.

Question: How does Java EE support DevOps practices?
Answer: Java EE integrates with CI/CD tools like Jenkins, Docker, and Kubernetes for automated deployment and scaling.

Question: What is the importance of resource pooling in Java EE?
Answer: Resource pooling improves performance by reusing connections, threads, and other resources.

Question: How does Java EE handle resource injection during deployment?
Answer: Resources like data sources, EJBs, and JMS queues are injected using annotations like @Resource.

Question: What is the significance of application server logs?
Answer: Server logs provide insights into deployment errors, performance issues, and application behavior.

Question: How do you handle versioning for Java EE applications?
Answer: Use version control systems like Git and maintain separate deployment packages for different versions.

Question: How do you deploy a Java EE microservice?
Answer: Package the microservice as a WAR or JAR and deploy it on a lightweight server or container like Docker.

Question: What is the difference between manual and automated deployment?

Answer: Manual deployment involves copying files and configurations manually, while automated deployment uses scripts and tools.

Question: How do you test a Java EE application post-deployment?
Answer: Perform functional, integration, and performance testing using tools like Selenium, JMeter, or Postman.

Question: How do you manage application downtime during deployment?
Answer: Use techniques like blue-green deployment or rolling updates to minimize downtime.

Question: What is rollback deployment in Java EE?
Answer: Rollback deployment restores a previous application version in case of deployment failures.

Question: How does Java EE support cloud deployment?
Answer: Java EE integrates with cloud platforms and container orchestration tools for scalable deployments.

Question: What are the best practices for deploying Java EE applications?
Answer: Use CI/CD pipelines, secure configurations, resource optimization, and monitoring tools for deployment.

Question: How do you ensure zero-downtime deployment in Java EE?
Answer: Use features like clustering, load balancing, and canary releases to ensure zero-downtime deployment.

3.6 Key Components of Java EE

Question: How does Java EE handle resource pooling?
Answer: Java EE manages resources like database connections and threads using resource pooling for performance optimization.

Question: What is the purpose of the Web Profile in Java EE?
Answer: The Web Profile is a lightweight subset of Java EE optimized for web applications.

Question: What is the role of the application server in Java EE?
Answer: The application server provides runtime environments, transaction management, and security for Java EE components.

Question: How does Java EE support RESTful web services?
Answer: Java EE uses JAX-RS for creating RESTful web services with annotations and automatic JSON/XML mapping.

Question: How does Java EE support SOAP-based web services?
Answer: Java EE uses JAX-WS for creating and consuming SOAP-based web services with WSDL support.

Question: What is the role of Managed Beans in Java EE?
Answer: Managed Beans provide lightweight components for managing business logic and dependencies.

Question: What is the JavaMail API in Java EE?
Answer: The JavaMail API enables sending and receiving emails from Java EE applications.

Question: What is the role of JNDI in Java EE?
Answer: JNDI (Java Naming and Directory Interface) is used to locate and access resources like data sources and EJBs.

Question: What is the advantage of using annotations in Java EE?
Answer: Annotations reduce configuration complexity by replacing XML-based descriptors.

Question: How does Java EE handle transactions?

Answer: Java EE supports container-managed and programmatic transactions to ensure data consistency.

Question: How does Java EE ensure security?
Answer: Java EE ensures security through role-based access control, secure communication, and JAAS.

Question: What is the role of the Servlet API in Java EE?
Answer: The Servlet API processes client requests and generates responses, forming the foundation of web applications.

Question: What is the purpose of the HTTP session in Java EE?
Answer: HTTP sessions track user interactions across multiple requests in a web application.

Question: How does Java EE handle resource injection?
Answer: Resources like data sources and EJBs are injected using annotations like @Resource and @EJB.

Question: How does Java EE support asynchronous operations?
Answer: Java EE supports asynchronous operations through JMS, asynchronous Servlets, and EJB timers.

Question: What is the significance of EAR files in Java EE?
Answer: EAR files package multiple Java EE modules (WAR, EJB, JAR) for deployment in enterprise applications.

Question: What is the role of the Persistence Context in JPA?
Answer: The Persistence Context manages the lifecycle of entity objects in a Java EE application.

Question: How does Java EE support microservices?
Answer: Java EE supports microservices with lightweight APIs like JAX-RS and containerized deployments.

Question: What is the role of the WebSocket API in modern applications?
Answer: The WebSocket API enables real-time communication, essential for chat, gaming, and live data updates.

Question: What are the advantages of using Java EE components?
Answer: Java EE components ensure modularity, scalability, portability, and robust security for enterprise applications.

Online Resources

	Practice Paper	**YouTube Video Playlist Link**
Link	https://forms.gle/EFRLye68mJB8KQof7	https://www.youtube.com/playlist?list=PLzlh_31VWEFpuOaJocdor00sKleSYUmnH
QR Code		

CHAPTER 4
Enterprise Application Development in Java

4.1 Leveraging Java EE for Enterprise Applications

Question: How does JAX-WS enable enterprise application integration?
Answer: JAX-WS supports SOAP-based web services, enabling integration with other enterprise systems.

Question: How does Java EE handle error management in enterprise applications?
Answer: Java EE uses exception handling, Interceptor APIs, and error pages to manage application errors.

Question: What is the purpose of EAR files in Java EE?
Answer: EAR (Enterprise Application Archive) files bundle multiple Java EE modules for deployment in enterprise environments.

Question: How does Java EE support asynchronous processing?
Answer: Java EE supports asynchronous processing using JMS, asynchronous Servlets, and EJB timers.

Question: What is the significance of resource pooling in Java EE?
Answer: Resource pooling optimizes performance by reusing database connections, threads, and other resources.

Question: How does Java EE ensure portability?
Answer: Java EE applications are portable across compliant application servers due to adherence to standard specifications.

Question: What is the role of Managed Beans in Java EE?
Answer: Managed Beans provide lightweight, reusable components for managing application logic and UI.

Question: How does Java EE simplify cloud deployment?
Answer: Java EE supports containerized deployments and integrates with cloud platforms for scalable and distributed applications.

Question: How does Java EE handle cross-cutting concerns?
Answer: Java EE uses Interceptors to address cross-cutting concerns like logging, security, and auditing.

Question: What is the importance of JNDI in enterprise applications?
Answer: JNDI simplifies resource lookup for databases, messaging queues, and EJBs in enterprise applications.

Question: How does Java EE support multi-tenancy in enterprise applications?
Answer: Java EE uses container features like resource isolation and custom configurations for multi-tenant environments.

Question: What is the role of the Deployment Descriptor?
Answer: Deployment Descriptors (e.g., web.xml) configure components, resources, and security settings for enterprise applications.

Question: How does Java EE ensure reliability in distributed systems?
Answer: Java EE ensures reliability through transaction management, exception handling, and monitoring tools.

Question: How does Java EE support DevOps practices?
Answer: Java EE integrates with CI/CD pipelines, container orchestration tools, and monitoring platforms for streamlined deployment.

Question: What is the significance of clustering in Java EE?

Answer: Clustering enables high availability and fault tolerance by distributing applications across multiple servers.

Question: How does Java EE handle resource injection?
Answer: Resources like data sources and EJBs are injected using annotations like @Resource and @EJB.

Question: How does Java EE support reporting in enterprise applications?
Answer: Java EE integrates with reporting tools and APIs for generating data-driven reports in enterprise systems.

Question: What is the significance of modular architecture in Java EE?
Answer: Modular architecture improves maintainability, scalability, and reusability in enterprise applications.

Question: How does Java EE manage database transactions?
Answer: Java EE manages database transactions using JTA and container-managed or programmatic transaction control.

Question: What are the advantages of leveraging Java EE for enterprise applications?
Answer: Java EE provides scalability, security, portability, modularity, and robust APIs for building enterprise-grade applications.

4.2 Design Patterns and Best Practices for Enterprise Development

Question: How is the Adapter pattern useful in enterprise development?
Answer: The Adapter pattern bridges incompatible interfaces, enabling components to work together seamlessly.

Question: What is the best practice for exception handling in Java EE?
Answer: Use centralized exception handling mechanisms, custom exception classes, and log errors for debugging.

Question: How do you ensure modularity in Java EE applications?
Answer: Use design patterns like MVC, DAO, and Session Facade to maintain clear separation of concerns and improve modularity.

Question: What is the advantage of using the Lazy Initialization pattern?
Answer: The Lazy Initialization pattern defers object creation until it is needed, improving performance and resource utilization.

Question: How does the Iterator pattern simplify collection traversal?
Answer: The Iterator pattern provides a way to access elements of a collection sequentially without exposing its underlying representation.

Question: How does the Flyweight pattern improve memory usage?
Answer: The Flyweight pattern minimizes memory usage by sharing common object states instead of creating new objects.

Question: What is the Chain of Responsibility pattern?
Answer: The Chain of Responsibility pattern passes a request along a chain of handlers until it is processed.

Question: How does the State pattern manage object behavior?
Answer: The State pattern allows an object to change its behavior when its internal state changes.

Question: What is the use of the Singleton pattern in Java EE services?
Answer: Singleton ensures a single instance of shared resources like caching mechanisms or configuration settings.

Question: How do you ensure code readability in enterprise applications?
Answer: Follow clean coding principles, meaningful variable names, and well-structured classes and methods.

Question: What is the benefit of using version control systems in Java EE development?
Answer: Version control systems like Git track changes, enable collaboration, and ensure rollback capabilities for enterprise projects.

Question: How do you optimize database queries in Java EE?
Answer: Use JPA query optimization techniques, indexing, and caching mechanisms to enhance database performance.

Question: What is the Repository pattern?
Answer: The Repository pattern abstracts data access logic, providing a cleaner separation between business logic and data persistence.

Question: What is the significance of automated testing in enterprise development?
Answer: Automated testing ensures application stability, detects bugs early, and reduces the cost of manual testing.

Question: How does the Observer pattern benefit event-driven systems?
Answer: It allows multiple observers to react to state changes, enabling efficient event handling in enterprise systems.

Question: What is the role of CI/CD in Java EE enterprise applications?
Answer: CI/CD automates building, testing, and deployment, ensuring faster and reliable releases.

Question: What are best practices for managing application configuration?
Answer: Use external configuration files, environment variables, and frameworks like Spring Boot for centralized configuration management.

Question: How does the Factory Method pattern improve object creation?
Answer: The Factory Method pattern delegates object creation to subclasses, promoting loose coupling.

Question: How does the Composite pattern handle hierarchical data?
Answer: The Composite pattern allows treating individual and composite objects uniformly, useful for hierarchical data structures.

Question: What are the key benefits of applying design patterns in enterprise applications?
Answer: Design patterns improve code reusability, maintainability, scalability, and adherence to best practices in enterprise applications.

4.3 Integration with External Systems and Services

Question: What is the importance of error handling in integration?
Answer: Error handling ensures reliability by managing communication failures, invalid data, and connection issues during integration.

Question: What is the use of JSON in system integration?
Answer: JSON is a lightweight data format widely used in RESTful APIs for data exchange between systems.

Question: How does Java EE handle XML-based integration?
Answer: Java EE provides APIs like JAXB for parsing, transforming, and generating XML during system integration.

Question: What is the role of webhooks in integration?

Answer: Webhooks enable real-time communication by allowing external systems to send HTTP callbacks when events occur.

Question: How does Java EE handle batch processing in integration?
Answer: Java EE uses the Batch API to process large volumes of data exchanged between systems in integration scenarios.

Question: What is the role of API gateways in integration?
Answer: API gateways manage API requests, routing, and security for seamless integration between Java EE applications and external APIs.

Question: What are the advantages of using REST APIs for integration?
Answer: REST APIs are lightweight, platform-independent, and easy to implement, making them ideal for system integration.

Question: How does Java EE handle versioning in system integration?
Answer: Use versioned endpoints in APIs and maintain backward compatibility to manage integration changes over time.

Question: How do you monitor integrations in Java EE?
Answer: Use monitoring tools, logging frameworks, and APM solutions like New Relic to track integration performance and errors.

Question: How does Java EE support message queuing in integration?
Answer: Java EE uses JMS to queue messages, ensuring reliable delivery in asynchronous system integration.

Question: What is the importance of data transformation in integration?
Answer: Data transformation ensures compatibility by converting data formats between integrated systems.

Question: What is the use of Swagger in integration?
Answer: Swagger provides API documentation, making it easier to integrate systems by understanding available endpoints and operations.

Question: How does Java EE support real-time integration?
Answer: Java EE supports real-time integration using WebSocket APIs or event-driven architectures.

Question: What is the significance of timeouts in integration?
Answer: Timeouts prevent indefinite waits and improve system reliability during integration by handling unresponsive external systems.

Question: What are the best practices for API integration?
Answer: Use standardized protocols, secure data exchange, versioning, and robust error handling for seamless API integration.

Question: How does Java EE support third-party payment gateway integration?
Answer: Java EE integrates with payment gateways using REST or SOAP APIs, along with secure authentication mechanisms.

Question: What is the role of OAuth in integration?
Answer: OAuth provides a secure mechanism for granting limited access to external systems without sharing credentials.

Question: How do you handle data consistency in integration?
Answer: Use distributed transactions, eventual consistency models, or conflict resolution strategies to ensure data integrity.

Question: How does Java EE handle state management in integration?
Answer: Java EE uses HTTP sessions, cookies, or JWT for managing state during system integration.

Question: What are the advantages of integrating external systems with Java EE?
Answer: Integration enhances functionality, automates workflows, and enables seamless data exchange between diverse systems.

4.4 Security in Java EE

Question: How does Java EE secure file uploads?
Answer: Java EE secures file uploads by validating file types, sizes, and paths, and storing files in secure locations.

Question: What is the role of security filters in Java EE?
Answer: Security filters intercept and process HTTP requests and responses to enforce security policies.

Question: How does Java EE implement two-factor authentication (2FA)?
Answer: Java EE integrates with external 2FA providers or implements custom 2FA mechanisms using OTPs or authentication apps.

Question: How does Java EE support secure API integration?
Answer: Java EE secures APIs with OAuth, API keys, and HTTPS to protect data and resources.

Question: What is the role of digital signatures in Java EE?
Answer: Digital signatures ensure data integrity and authenticity in Java EE applications by verifying the sender.

Question: How does Java EE handle user identity propagation?
Answer: Java EE propagates user identity across components using JAAS or container-managed security contexts.

Question: How does Java EE secure microservices?
Answer: Java EE secures microservices using OAuth, mutual TLS, and API gateways.

Question: How does Java EE prevent directory traversal attacks?
Answer: Java EE prevents directory traversal by validating input paths and restricting access to unauthorized directories.

Question: What is the role of PKI in Java EE security?
Answer: PKI (Public Key Infrastructure) enables secure key exchange and digital certificate management in Java EE applications.

Question: How does Java EE handle error message security?
Answer: Java EE masks sensitive error details to prevent information leakage to potential attackers.

Question: How do you configure HTTPS in a Java EE application server?
Answer: Configure HTTPS by generating SSL certificates, enabling secure connectors, and updating application URLs.

Question: How does Java EE secure session cookies?
Answer: Java EE secures session cookies by setting HttpOnly and Secure flags and enabling SameSite attributes.

Question: What is the role of a security manager in Java EE?
Answer: The security manager enforces access control policies for Java code running in the application.

Question: How does Java EE handle password policies?
Answer: Java EE enforces password policies through validation, complexity requirements, and expiration rules.

Question: What is mutual TLS in Java EE?
Answer: Mutual TLS authenticates both client and server, ensuring secure two-way communication.

Question: How does Java EE prevent brute force attacks?
Answer: Java EE prevents brute force attacks by implementing account lockouts, CAPTCHA, and monitoring failed login attempts.

Question: How does Java EE secure cloud-based applications?
Answer: Java EE secures cloud applications with encrypted communication, identity federation, and compliance with cloud security standards.

Question: What is the importance of auditing in Java EE security?
Answer: Auditing tracks security events, detects anomalies, and ensures compliance with security policies.

Question: How does Java EE support secure logging?
Answer: Java EE integrates with secure logging frameworks to store logs in an encrypted and tamper-proof manner.

Question: What are the best practices for securing Java EE applications?
Answer: Use HTTPS, secure authentication, role-based access control, and regular vulnerability assessments for secure Java EE applications.

4.5 Enterprise Application Design Patterns

Question: How is the Proxy pattern used in enterprise applications?
Answer: The Proxy pattern controls access to an object, adding functionality like lazy initialization or security checks.

Question: What is the Flyweight pattern?
Answer: The Flyweight pattern minimizes memory usage by sharing common object states.

Question: What is the State pattern?
Answer: The State pattern allows an object to change its behavior when its state changes.

Question: How is the Repository pattern implemented in enterprise applications?
Answer: The Repository pattern abstracts data access logic, providing a clean API for interacting with the persistence layer.

Question: What is the Lazy Initialization pattern?
Answer: The Lazy Initialization pattern defers object creation until it is needed, optimizing resource usage.

Question: What is the Iterator pattern?
Answer: The Iterator pattern provides a way to sequentially access elements in a collection without exposing its internal structure.

Question: What is the Dependency Injection pattern?
Answer: Dependency Injection simplifies dependency management by allowing containers to inject required objects automatically.

Question: What is the Observer pattern's role in event-driven systems?
Answer: It enables multiple components to react to changes in the state of a single component, supporting event-driven programming.

Question: What is the Active Record pattern?

Answer: The Active Record pattern integrates data access logic into domain objects, simplifying CRUD operations.

Question: How is the Template Pattern used in data processing?
Answer: It defines the steps of a process, allowing subclasses to provide custom implementations for specific steps.

Question: What is the Façade pattern in Java EE?
Answer: The Façade pattern provides a simplified interface to a complex subsystem, reducing coupling.

Question: What is the Null Object pattern?
Answer: The Null Object pattern provides a default behavior for null references, avoiding null checks.

Question: What is the benefit of using design patterns in enterprise applications?
Answer: Design patterns promote reusable, maintainable, and scalable solutions for common architectural problems.

Question: How does the Factory pattern enhance flexibility?
Answer: It decouples object creation from the client, allowing the dynamic selection of concrete classes.

Question: What is the use of the Composite pattern?
Answer: The Composite pattern treats individual objects and compositions uniformly, useful for hierarchical structures.

Question: How does the Observer pattern promote decoupling?
Answer: Observers register with a subject and are notified of changes, reducing dependencies between components.

Question: What is the importance of the Service Layer pattern?
Answer: The Service Layer pattern centralizes business logic, promoting separation of concerns.

Question: How does the Bridge pattern work in Java EE?
Answer: The Bridge pattern separates abstraction from implementation, allowing them to evolve independently.

Question: What is the Double-Checked Locking pattern?
Answer: This pattern ensures thread-safe Singleton initialization with minimal synchronization overhead.

Question: What is the importance of applying best practices with design patterns?
Answer: Best practices ensure that design patterns are applied appropriately, improving code quality and system performance.

4.6 Testing and Debugging

Question: How is UI testing performed in Java applications?
Answer: Tools like Selenium and JavaFX Test are used for automated testing of graphical user interfaces.

Question: What is a stack trace?
Answer: A stack trace is a report of the execution stack at a specific point, showing the sequence of method calls leading to an error.

Question: What is black-box testing?
Answer: Black-box testing validates application functionality without knowledge of the internal code or implementation.

Question: What is white-box testing?
Answer: White-box testing examines the internal logic, code paths, and algorithms of the application.

Question: How does continuous integration (CI) support testing?
Answer: CI automates testing as part of the build process, ensuring that code changes are tested before merging.

Question: What is the purpose of debugging tools like Eclipse Debugger?
Answer: Debugging tools provide graphical interfaces for setting breakpoints, inspecting variables, and stepping through code.

Question: How does static code analysis assist in testing?
Answer: Static code analysis tools like SonarQube detect coding errors, security vulnerabilities, and maintainability issues.

Question: What is smoke testing?
Answer: Smoke testing verifies that the basic functionality of an application is working after a new build or deployment.

Question: What is the difference between debugging and testing?
Answer: Testing identifies defects, while debugging locates and fixes the defects in the code.

Question: How does load testing differ from stress testing?
Answer: Load testing evaluates performance under expected load, while stress testing measures performance under extreme load.

Question: What is the role of a bug tracking system?
Answer: Bug tracking systems like Jira track, prioritize, and manage reported defects during development.

Question: How does version control support debugging?
Answer: Version control systems like Git allow developers to track changes, identify regressions, and revert to stable states.

Question: What are test suites in JUnit?
Answer: Test suites group multiple test cases for execution, enabling comprehensive testing of related functionality.

Question: How do you handle intermittent bugs?
Answer: Use logging, monitoring, and stress testing to identify conditions that trigger intermittent bugs.

Question: What is exploratory testing?
Answer: Exploratory testing involves simultaneously learning and testing the application to identify unexpected issues.

Question: How does thread dump analysis assist debugging?
Answer: Thread dumps provide insights into thread states and activity, helping diagnose deadlocks and performance issues.

Question: What is a memory leak, and how do you debug it?
Answer: A memory leak occurs when unused objects are not garbage collected. Tools like VisualVM help identify and fix leaks.

Question: How does code refactoring improve testing?
Answer: Refactoring improves code readability and maintainability, making it easier to write effective tests.

Question: How do you perform database testing?
Answer: Use tools like DbUnit or direct queries to validate data integrity, schema, and stored procedures in the database.

Question: What are best practices for testing and debugging Java applications?
Answer: Use automated tests, maintain clean code, log effectively, handle exceptions properly, and continuously monitor application behavior.

4.7 Deployment and Packaging

Question: How does Java EE support cloud deployment?
Answer: Java EE applications can be deployed on cloud platforms using container orchestration tools like Kubernetes and Docker.

Question: What is the importance of resource pooling during deployment?
Answer: Resource pooling optimizes performance by reusing database connections, threads, and other resources.

Question: How do you monitor deployed applications?
Answer: Use application server tools, logging frameworks, and monitoring solutions like JMX or APM tools.

Question: How does Java EE handle security during deployment?
Answer: Java EE uses role-based access control, secure configurations, and HTTPS for securing deployed applications.

Question: What is a context root in deployment?
Answer: The context root defines the URL prefix for accessing a deployed web application.

Question: How do you deploy microservices in Java EE?
Answer: Package microservices as lightweight WAR or JAR files and deploy them on a containerized platform or lightweight server.

Question: What is the significance of versioning in deployment?
Answer: Versioning ensures backward compatibility and facilitates the management of multiple application versions.

Question: How do you rollback a deployment?
Answer: Use server tools or scripts to redeploy the previous application version in case of deployment failures.

Question: What is a deployment pipeline?
Answer: A deployment pipeline automates building, testing, and deploying applications, ensuring faster and reliable releases.

Question: What is the role of CI/CD in Java EE deployment?
Answer: CI/CD automates integration, testing, and deployment, improving the speed and reliability of application delivery.

Question: How does Java EE support multi-tenancy during deployment?
Answer: Java EE uses configuration isolation and resource partitioning to support multi-tenant environments.

Question: What are the best practices for deploying Java EE applications?
Answer: Use automated pipelines, secure configurations, versioning, and monitoring for effective deployment.

Question: What is artifact repository management in deployment?
Answer: Tools like Nexus and Artifactory store and manage deployable artifacts, ensuring efficient dependency resolution.

Question: How does Java EE handle externalized configurations?
Answer: Externalized configurations are managed using environment-specific files or tools like Spring Cloud Config.

Question: What is the role of orchestration in deployment?
Answer: Orchestration tools like Kubernetes manage the deployment, scaling, and monitoring of containerized Java EE applications.

Question: How does Java EE support disaster recovery in deployment?
Answer: Use backups, failover mechanisms, and distributed architectures to ensure data integrity and application availability.

Question: What is the importance of hotfix deployment?
Answer: Hotfix deployment addresses critical issues without waiting for the next release cycle, minimizing downtime.

Question: How do you manage secrets in Java EE deployment?
Answer: Use secure storage solutions like Vault or server-native key management to manage sensitive data like API keys.

Question: What is the difference between manual and automated deployment?
Answer: Manual deployment requires human intervention, while automated deployment uses scripts and tools for faster and error-free deployment.

Question: How do you ensure deployment success?
Answer: Test thoroughly, monitor logs, automate pipelines, and use rollback strategies to ensure successful deployments.

4.8 Case Studies and Real-World Examples

Question: How does Java EE handle integration with legacy systems?
Answer: Java EE uses the Connector API and web services to integrate seamlessly with legacy systems in real-world scenarios.

Question: How was Java EE implemented in a payment gateway?
Answer: Java EE enabled secure transaction processing, fraud detection, and API integration for third-party payment solutions.

Question: How does Java EE power ERP systems?
Answer: ERP systems use Java EE for managing modules like HR, finance, and inventory with scalability and robust security.

Question: What is a practical application of Java EE in the travel industry?
Answer: Travel platforms use Java EE for itinerary planning, booking systems, and integrating with hotel and airline APIs.

Question: How does Java EE support AI-driven enterprise solutions?
Answer: Java EE integrates with AI libraries and frameworks for predictive analytics, chatbots, and automated decision-making.

Question: What is a case study of Java EE in fraud detection?
Answer: A financial application used Java EE to integrate machine learning algorithms for real-time fraud detection.

Question: How does Java EE handle real-time notifications?
Answer: Java EE uses JMS and WebSocket APIs for sending real-time notifications in enterprise applications.

Question: How is Java EE applied in digital marketing platforms?
Answer: Digital marketing platforms use Java EE for campaign management, analytics, and multi-channel integrations.

Question: How does Java EE support blockchain applications?
Answer: Java EE integrates with blockchain APIs for secure transactions and decentralized record management.

Question: How was Java EE used in a ticketing system?
Answer: Java EE enabled a real-time ticketing system with features for seat selection, dynamic pricing, and secure payments.

Question: What is the role of Java EE in supply chain optimization?
Answer: Java EE supports optimization by integrating IoT devices, automating workflows, and providing real-time data visibility.

Question: How was Java EE implemented in a hospitality management system?
Answer: Java EE powered room booking, guest management, and personalized services in a hotel chain's system.

Question: How does Java EE support fintech applications?
Answer: Fintech applications use Java EE for secure payments, regulatory compliance, and scalable infrastructure.

Question: How was Java EE applied in a learning management system (LMS)?
Answer: Java EE enabled online course delivery, user role management, and progress tracking in an LMS.

Question: How does Java EE integrate with third-party APIs?
Answer: Java EE uses REST and SOAP web services to communicate with third-party APIs in real-world applications.

Question: What is a case study of Java EE in retail analytics?
Answer: A retail platform used Java EE for customer behavior analysis, inventory forecasting, and targeted marketing campaigns.

Question: How is Java EE used in social media platforms?
Answer: Java EE powers features like user authentication, content sharing, and real-time messaging in social media applications.

Question: How does Java EE support DevOps practices in real-world projects?
Answer: Java EE integrates with CI/CD pipelines, containerization tools, and monitoring solutions for seamless DevOps workflows.

Question: What is a real-world use case of Java EE in the gaming industry?
Answer: Java EE supports multiplayer gaming with real-time server communication, user authentication, and game state management.

Question: How does Java EE enhance user experience in enterprise applications?
Answer: Java EE provides frameworks for responsive design, secure interactions, and fast data processing, improving user experience.

Online Resources

	Practice Paper	YouTube Video Playlist Link
Link	https://forms.gle/1dVqBZ4UM6HAnLU18	https://www.youtube.com/playlist?list=PLzlh_31VWEFokCbKSWCTyPylh8zmCWzTr
QR Code		

CHAPTER 5
Building and Deploying JAR and WAR Files

5.1 Building JAR Files: Compiling Java Source Code, Packaging Resources

Question: What is a "fat" JAR file?
Answer: A fat JAR file bundles the application along with all its dependencies into a single archive.

Question: How do you debug a JAR file?
Answer: Use debugging tools and commands like java -jar fileName.jar with logging enabled or by attaching a debugger.

Question: How do you verify the contents of a JAR file?
Answer: Use the jar tf fileName.jar command to list the contents and ensure all required files are included.

Question: Can a JAR file contain other JAR files?
Answer: Yes, a JAR can include other JARs, but their class paths must be configured correctly.

Question: What is the purpose of signing a JAR file?
Answer: Signing a JAR file ensures its authenticity and integrity by verifying the source of the code.

Question: How do you sign a JAR file?
Answer: Use the jarsigner tool to sign a JAR file with a digital certificate.

Question: How do you create a manifest file for a JAR file?
Answer: Use a text editor to create the file with attributes like Main-Class and save it as MANIFEST.MF.

Question: What is the difference between a library JAR and an executable JAR?
Answer: A library JAR contains reusable classes, while an executable JAR contains a Main-Class entry for execution.

Question: How do you handle large applications with multiple JARs?
Answer: Use a Class-Path entry in the manifest file or a build tool like Maven to manage dependencies.

Question: How do you create a JAR file with Maven?
Answer: Use the Maven package command, which builds the application and generates a JAR file in the target directory.

Question: What is the role of Gradle in building JAR files?
Answer: Gradle automates the process of compiling, testing, and packaging JAR files with flexible build scripts.

Question: Can a JAR file run on any platform?
Answer: Yes, as long as the target platform has a compatible Java Runtime Environment (JRE).

Question: What is the purpose of a dependency JAR?
Answer: A dependency JAR contains external libraries required by the application.

Question: How do you optimize a JAR file for deployment?
Answer: Remove unnecessary files, minimize dependencies, and ensure the MANIFEST.MF file is properly configured.

Question: How does a JAR file handle versioning?
Answer: Use metadata entries in the MANIFEST.MF file to specify version details.

Question: How do you test a JAR file?

Answer: Run the JAR file using java -jar and test its functionality with the required input or configuration.

Question: Can a JAR file contain native libraries?
Answer: Yes, native libraries can be included in a JAR file, but they need to be extracted and loaded separately.

Question: How do you ensure compatibility of a JAR file?
Answer: Use the same or compatible Java version during compilation and runtime to avoid compatibility issues.

Question: How do you add metadata to a JAR file?
Answer: Include metadata in the MANIFEST.MF file or additional configuration files inside the META-INF directory.

Question: What are the best practices for building JAR files?
Answer: Use a build tool, test thoroughly, include a clear MANIFEST.MF file, and ensure all dependencies are resolved.

5.2 Building WAR Files: Assembling Web Application Resources, Packaging

Question: How do you configure session timeout in a WAR file?
Answer: Set the session timeout in the web.xml file using the <session-timeout> element.

Question: Can a WAR file contain EJBs?
Answer: No, EJBs are packaged in JAR files within an EAR file for enterprise applications, not directly in a WAR.

Question: What is the Class-Path entry in the manifest of a WAR file?
Answer: The Class-Path entry specifies paths to external libraries needed by the web application.

Question: How do you handle versioning for a WAR file?
Answer: Include version details in the file name or in the metadata of the web.xml file for better management.

Question: How do you deploy multiple WAR files on the same server?
Answer: Place each WAR file in the server's deployment directory; each will have its own context root.

Question: How do you configure logging in a WAR file?
Answer: Add logging configurations in the WEB-INF/classes directory or externalize it for better control.

Question: What is a context root in a WAR file?
Answer: The context root is the base URL path through which a web application is accessed on a server.

Question: How do you secure a WAR file?
Answer: Use HTTPS, define security roles in web.xml, and include only necessary resources in the WAR.

Question: How do you update a WAR file on a server?
Answer: Replace the existing WAR file in the deployment directory or redeploy it using the admin console.

Question: How do you include third-party libraries in a WAR file?
Answer: Place third-party libraries in the WEB-INF/lib directory.

Question: What tools can automate WAR file packaging?
Answer: Tools like Maven, Gradle, and Ant automate the process of building and packaging WAR files.

Question: How do you debug a deployed WAR file?
Answer: Enable logging, use server logs, and attach a remote debugger to the application server.

Question: How do you externalize configurations in a WAR file?

Answer: Use properties files or environment variables to manage configurations outside the WAR file.

Question: How do you handle multi-module projects in WAR packaging?
Answer: Use a build tool like Maven or Gradle to package the web module as a WAR and other modules as dependencies.

Question: What is a lightweight WAR file?
Answer: A lightweight WAR file excludes unnecessary resources and externalizes dependencies for optimized deployment.

Question: How does a WAR file integrate with databases?
Answer: Configure database connections in web.xml or use JNDI resources provided by the application server.

Question: How do you set up a build pipeline for WAR files?
Answer: Use CI/CD tools like Jenkins or GitHub Actions to automate building, testing, and deploying WAR files.

Question: What is the importance of dependency management in WAR files?
Answer: Proper dependency management ensures the application runs smoothly without missing or conflicting libraries.

Question: How do you ensure a WAR file is platform-independent?
Answer: Use platform-independent libraries and ensure compliance with Java EE specifications.

Question: What are the best practices for building and deploying WAR files?
Answer: Automate builds, externalize configurations, secure resources, and test thoroughly before deployment.

5.3 Deploying JAR Files: Executing Standalone Applications

Question: How do you ensure secure deployment of JAR files?
Answer: Sign the JAR file, use secure communication protocols, and validate inputs to prevent vulnerabilities.

Question: How do you handle versioning for JAR files?
Answer: Include version information in the file name or the MANIFEST.MF file.

Question: How do you deploy a JAR file in a containerized environment?
Answer: Package the JAR file in a Docker image with a compatible JRE and deploy the container.

Question: What is the significance of the META-INF directory in a JAR file?
Answer: The META-INF directory contains the manifest file and metadata required for JAR execution.

Question: How do you verify a signed JAR file?
Answer: Use the jarsigner -verify command to check the integrity and authenticity of the signed JAR.

Question: How do you handle large JAR files with multiple dependencies?
Answer: Use build tools like Maven or Gradle to manage dependencies and create optimized packages.

Question: Can a JAR file run without a JRE?
Answer: No, a JAR file requires a compatible Java Runtime Environment to execute.

Question: How do you optimize a JAR file for deployment?
Answer: Remove unused classes, minimize dependencies, and compress the JAR to reduce its size.

Question: How do you update a deployed JAR file?
Answer: Replace the old JAR file with the new version and restart the application if necessary.

Question: How do you create a manifest file for a JAR file?
Answer: Use a text editor to create the MANIFEST.MF file with entries like Main-Class and include it during JAR creation.

Question: What are the limitations of a JAR file?
Answer: JAR files are not ideal for large-scale applications requiring modular architecture or complex dependency management.

Question: How do you externalize dependencies for a JAR file?
Answer: Use the Class-Path attribute in the manifest file to specify external dependency locations.

Question: How do you test a standalone JAR file?
Answer: Use unit tests, integration tests, and test execution with the java -jar command in different environments.

Question: What tools help automate the deployment of JAR files?
Answer: CI/CD tools like Jenkins, GitHub Actions, or Docker help automate building and deploying JAR files.

Question: How do you configure JVM options for a JAR application?
Answer: Pass JVM options like -Xmx or -Xms before the -jar option in the execution command.

Question: Can a JAR file contain multiple Main-Class entries?
Answer: No, a JAR file can only specify one Main-Class in the manifest for execution. Others can be invoked programmatically.

Question: How do you deploy a JAR file for distributed applications?
Answer: Use distributed systems tools like Apache Kafka or Hadoop to manage the execution of JAR files across nodes.

Question: How do you include logging frameworks in a JAR file?
Answer: Package logging frameworks in the JAR or use external configurations like log4j.properties for runtime logging.

Question: What are the benefits of deploying a standalone JAR file?
Answer: Standalone JARs are easy to deploy, portable, and self-contained, reducing deployment complexity.

Question: What are the best practices for deploying JAR files?
Answer: Test thoroughly, include necessary dependencies, sign the JAR, and document execution steps clearly.

5.4 Deploying WAR Files: Deploying Web Applications to Java EE Application Servers

Question: How do you deploy a WAR file to WildFly or JBoss?
Answer: Use the deploy command in the CLI or copy the WAR file to the deployment directory.

Question: What is the purpose of filters in a WAR file?
Answer: Filters preprocess or postprocess requests and responses, such as for logging or authentication.

Question: How does the Class-Path entry in the manifest file affect deployment?
Answer: It specifies the paths to external libraries needed by the application during runtime.

Question: How do you handle configuration changes for a deployed WAR file?
Answer: Use external configuration files or environment variables to modify settings without changing the WAR.

Question: How do you monitor a deployed WAR application?
Answer: Use server-provided monitoring tools, logs, or third-party solutions like New Relic.

Question: How do you manage resources in a WAR file?
Answer: Place static resources like images and CSS in directories accessible via the application's context root.

Question: How do you configure security roles for a WAR file?
Answer: Define roles in the web.xml file and map them to users or groups in the application server.

Question: What is the purpose of session persistence in WAR deployment?
Answer: Session persistence ensures that user sessions remain intact during server restarts or crashes.

Question: How do you deploy a WAR file in a clustered environment?
Answer: Configure the cluster in the application server and deploy the WAR file to each node.

Question: How do you configure context parameters in a WAR file?
Answer: Define context parameters in the web.xml file using the <context-param> tag.

Question: How does a WAR file handle internationalization (i18n)?
Answer: Include resource bundles in the WEB-INF/classes directory and use Java's i18n APIs.

Question: How do you deploy a WAR file on cloud platforms?
Answer: Use services like AWS Elastic Beanstalk or Azure App Service to deploy WAR files directly.

Question: How do you ensure zero-downtime deployment for a WAR file?
Answer: Use techniques like blue-green deployment or rolling updates in a clustered environment.

Question: What is a lightweight WAR file?
Answer: A lightweight WAR excludes unnecessary resources and externalizes configurations for better performance.

Question: How do you secure communications for a deployed WAR application?
Answer: Use HTTPS with SSL/TLS certificates and configure the server to enforce secure communication.

Question: How do you rollback a deployed WAR file?
Answer: Redeploy the previous version of the WAR file and restart the application if needed.

Question: How do you set up a deployment pipeline for WAR files?
Answer: Use CI/CD tools like Jenkins or GitHub Actions to automate build, test, and deployment processes.

Question: How do you externalize database configurations in WAR deployment?
Answer: Use JNDI data sources configured on the server, referenced in the web.xml file.

Question: How do you troubleshoot issues with a deployed WAR file?
Answer: Check server logs, verify configurations, and test the application endpoints to identify problems.

Question: What are the best practices for deploying WAR files?
Answer: Automate deployment, use version control, secure resources, test thoroughly, and monitor applications in production.

Online Resources

	Practice Paper	YouTube Video Playlist Link
Link	https://forms.gle/4bfqqAKSv2Yrb65v8	https://www.youtube.com/playlist?list=PLzlh_31VWEFpMZfsWV2xV3X89dvL3CFJd
QR Code		

CHAPTER 6
Basics of Web Application Development

6.1 What is a Web Application?

Question: What is a web application framework?
Answer: A web application framework simplifies development by providing pre-built modules and tools for building web applications, e.g., Spring and Django.

Question: How do web applications ensure security?
Answer: Web applications use HTTPS, authentication, authorization, input validation, and encryption to ensure security.

Question: What is a cookie in a web application?
Answer: A cookie is a small piece of data stored on the client's browser to maintain session state or preferences.

Question: What is a session in web applications?
Answer: A session tracks user interactions with a web application, maintaining state across multiple requests.

Question: What is the difference between GET and POST requests?
Answer: GET requests retrieve data, while POST requests send data to the server for processing.

Question: What is the importance of responsiveness in web applications?
Answer: Responsive design ensures that web applications work seamlessly on different devices and screen sizes.

Question: What is the role of JavaScript in web applications?
Answer: JavaScript enables interactive and dynamic user interfaces by manipulating the DOM and handling events.

Question: How do web applications handle scalability?
Answer: Scalability is achieved through load balancing, caching, database optimization, and horizontal scaling of servers.

Question: What is an example of a web application?
Answer: Examples include Gmail (email), Amazon (e-commerce), and Netflix (streaming service).

Question: What is the difference between a website and a web application?
Answer: Websites provide static information, while web applications allow user interaction and perform dynamic tasks.

Question: What is a hybrid web application?
Answer: A hybrid web application combines features of both web and native applications, often using technologies like React Native.

Question: What is the role of CSS in web applications?
Answer: CSS styles the user interface, enhancing the visual presentation of web applications.

Question: How do microservices integrate with web applications?
Answer: Web applications use APIs to interact with microservices, enabling modular and scalable architecture.

Question: What is the purpose of a CDN in web applications?
Answer: A Content Delivery Network (CDN) distributes static assets, reducing latency and improving performance.

Question: How do web applications use AJAX?

Answer: AJAX enables asynchronous data exchange with the server, allowing dynamic updates without reloading the page.

Question: What is the role of HTTPS in web applications?
Answer: HTTPS encrypts communication between the client and server, ensuring data integrity and security.

Question: What is the importance of user authentication in web applications?
Answer: Authentication verifies the user's identity, ensuring secure access to web application features.

Question: What are the challenges of web application development?
Answer: Challenges include security risks, cross-browser compatibility, performance optimization, and maintaining scalability.

Question: How do RESTful web services integrate with web applications?
Answer: RESTful web services provide stateless APIs for web applications to exchange data with servers or other systems.

Question: What are the advantages of cloud-based web applications?
Answer: Cloud-based web applications offer scalability, reliability, and ease of access without requiring local resources.

6.2 Understanding Web Clients and Servers

Question: What is caching in web communication?
Answer: Caching stores copies of frequently accessed data to reduce latency and improve client-server performance.

Question: How do RESTful web services work in client-server communication?
Answer: RESTful services use HTTP methods like GET, POST, PUT, and DELETE to exchange data between clients and servers in a stateless manner.

Question: What is a session in web applications?
Answer: A session maintains user-specific data across multiple requests during a user's interaction with a web application.

Question: What is the role of headers in HTTP communication?
Answer: HTTP headers provide metadata about the request or response, such as content type, encoding, and authorization.

Question: What is the purpose of a 301 redirect?
Answer: A 301 redirect indicates a permanent move of a resource to a new URL, directing clients to the updated location.

Question: What is the importance of middleware in client-server communication?
Answer: Middleware processes requests and responses between clients and servers, handling tasks like authentication and data transformation.

Question: How do web servers serve static files?
Answer: Web servers serve static files directly from the file system without invoking any backend processing.

Question: What is an API gateway in client-server architecture?
Answer: An API gateway manages client requests and routes them to appropriate microservices or backend systems.

Question: What is server-side rendering (SSR)?

Answer: SSR generates HTML content on the server before sending it to the client, improving SEO and initial load times.

Question: What is client-side rendering (CSR)?
Answer: CSR uses JavaScript to build the user interface dynamically in the client's browser, reducing server workload.

Question: How do web servers handle HTTPS connections?
Answer: Web servers use SSL/TLS certificates to encrypt data, ensuring secure communication between the client and server.

Question: What is a virtual host in web servers?
Answer: Virtual hosting allows multiple domains or websites to be hosted on a single web server.

Question: How do web clients handle redirects?
Answer: Web clients follow HTTP status codes like 301 or 302 to automatically request the new resource location.

Question: What is a REST API client?
Answer: A REST API client sends HTTP requests to RESTful services and processes the responses, often used for testing or integrations.

Question: What is the difference between synchronous and asynchronous requests?
Answer: Synchronous requests block further execution until a response is received, while asynchronous requests allow other tasks to continue.

Question: What is the role of a CDN in client-server communication?
Answer: A CDN (Content Delivery Network) accelerates content delivery by caching data on geographically distributed servers.

Question: How do modern web servers handle scalability?
Answer: Modern web servers use clustering, containerization, and load balancers to manage scalability and high traffic.

Question: What is a 503 Service Unavailable error?
Answer: A 503 error indicates that the server is temporarily unable to handle the request, often due to maintenance or overload.

Question: What is a web application firewall (WAF)?
Answer: A WAF protects web applications from malicious traffic by filtering and monitoring HTTP requests.

Question: What are best practices for client-server communication?
Answer: Use secure protocols (HTTPS), implement proper error handling, cache frequently used data, and optimize requests.

6.3 Key Components of Web Applications

Question: What is a RESTful API?
Answer: A RESTful API uses HTTP methods and principles of REST to facilitate communication between components.

Question: What is GraphQL in web applications?
Answer: GraphQL is a query language for APIs that allows clients to request specific data, reducing over-fetching.

Question: How do stateful and stateless components differ?

Answer: Stateful components maintain user session data, while stateless components do not retain information between requests.

Question: What is the role of JavaScript frameworks in web applications?
Answer: Frameworks like React and Angular simplify the development of dynamic and interactive frontend components.

Question: How do web applications use AJAX?
Answer: AJAX enables asynchronous data exchange with the server, updating the page content without reloading.

Question: What is a service worker in web applications?
Answer: A service worker is a script that runs in the background, enabling offline capabilities and caching.

Question: How do web applications manage user sessions?
Answer: Sessions are managed using cookies, tokens, or server-side session stores.

Question: What is the MVC architecture?
Answer: The MVC (Model-View-Controller) architecture separates data (Model), UI (View), and logic (Controller) for modular design.

Question: What is a backend framework?
Answer: Backend frameworks like Spring or Django provide tools for building robust and scalable server-side applications.

Question: How do web applications handle scalability?
Answer: Scalability is managed through load balancing, horizontal scaling, and database optimization.

Question: What is the importance of a build tool in web applications?
Answer: Build tools like Maven or Webpack automate tasks like compilation, packaging, and dependency management.

Question: How does HTTPS secure web applications?
Answer: HTTPS encrypts communication between the client and server, ensuring data integrity and privacy.

Question: What is the role of input validation in web applications?
Answer: Input validation prevents security vulnerabilities like SQL injection and XSS by sanitizing user input.

Question: What is serverless architecture?
Answer: Serverless architecture allows developers to build and run applications without managing servers, using cloud services.

Question: How do web applications use webhooks?
Answer: Webhooks send real-time data from one application to another based on specific events or triggers.

Question: What is the difference between SQL and NoSQL databases?
Answer: SQL databases use structured schemas, while NoSQL databases are flexible and ideal for unstructured data.

Question: What is a message queue in web applications?
Answer: A message queue manages asynchronous communication between application components, improving scalability and reliability.

Question: What is cross-origin resource sharing (CORS)?
Answer: CORS is a security feature that allows or restricts resources on a web server to be accessed from different origins.

Question: How do microservices benefit web applications?
Answer: Microservices enhance scalability, flexibility, and maintainability by breaking applications into smaller, independent services.

Question: What are the best practices for designing web application components?
Answer: Best practices include modular design, secure coding, efficient caching, and responsive frontend development.

6.4 HTTP Protocol Basics

Question: What are the main parts of an HTTP request?
Answer: An HTTP request consists of a request line (method, URI, version), headers, and an optional body.

Question: What is the role of the Content-Type header?
Answer: The Content-Type header specifies the format of the request or response body, such as JSON or XML.

Question: What is the Accept header in HTTP?
Answer: The Accept header indicates the media types that the client can handle, such as application/json.

Question: What is HTTP keep-alive?
Answer: HTTP keep-alive allows multiple requests and responses to be sent over a single connection, reducing overhead.

Question: What is the role of the Authorization header in HTTP?
Answer: The Authorization header provides credentials for authenticating the client with the server.

Question: What is the difference between idempotent and non-idempotent methods in HTTP?
Answer: Idempotent methods (e.g., GET, PUT) produce the same result regardless of repetitions, while non-idempotent methods (e.g., POST) may change state.

Question: What is the User-Agent header?
Answer: The User-Agent header identifies the client application making the request, such as a browser or API client.

Question: What is a RESTful HTTP API?
Answer: A RESTful HTTP API uses HTTP methods and principles of REST to enable stateless client-server communication.

Question: What are cache control headers in HTTP?
Answer: Cache control headers, such as Cache-Control and Expires, manage how responses are cached by clients and intermediaries.

Question: What is a 404 error in HTTP?
Answer: A 404 error indicates that the server cannot find the requested resource.

Question: What is a 500 error in HTTP?
Answer: A 500 error signifies an internal server error, often caused by misconfigurations or runtime exceptions.

Question: What is the difference between PUT and PATCH methods?
Answer: The PUT method replaces the entire resource, while PATCH updates only specific fields of a resource.

Question: What is cross-origin resource sharing (CORS)?
Answer: CORS is a security feature that allows or restricts resources on a web server to be accessed from a different origin.

Question: What is the role of the Referer header?
Answer: The Referer header provides the URL of the resource that referred the client to the current request.

Question: What is a 401 status code in HTTP?
Answer: A 401 status code indicates that authentication is required but has not been provided or is invalid.

Question: How does HTTP handle large file uploads?
Answer: HTTP supports large file uploads using chunked transfer encoding or multipart form data.

Question: What is the difference between persistent and non-persistent connections in HTTP?
Answer: Persistent connections remain open for multiple requests, while non-persistent connections close after each request-response cycle.

Question: What is a 403 status code?
Answer: A 403 status code indicates that the server understands the request but refuses to authorize it.

Question: What is the difference between HTTP and WebSockets?
Answer: HTTP is request-response-based, while WebSockets enable full-duplex communication between client and server.

Question: What is the ETag header in HTTP?
Answer: The ETag header provides a unique identifier for a resource, enabling efficient caching and validation.

6.5 Introduction to HTML

Question: What is the role of the <iframe> tag?
Answer: The <iframe> tag embeds another HTML document within the current page.

Question: What is the difference between HTML4 and HTML5?
Answer: HTML5 introduces new elements (e.g., <video>, <canvas>) and APIs, while HTML4 lacks these modern features.

Question: What is the purpose of the <nav> tag?
Answer: The <nav> tag defines navigation links, improving the structure and semantics of a web page.

Question: What is the <audio> tag used for?
Answer: The <audio> tag embeds audio content in a web page, with controls for playback.

Question: How do you include comments in HTML?
Answer: Use <!-- comment --> to add comments that are not displayed on the web page.

Question: What is the <canvas> tag?
Answer: The <canvas> tag provides a drawing area for graphics using JavaScript.

Question: How do you create a dropdown list in HTML?
Answer: Use the <select> element with nested <option> tags for dropdown menus.

Question: What is the <footer> tag used for?
Answer: The <footer> tag defines the footer section of a web page, typically containing copyright or contact information.

Question: What is the purpose of the id attribute in HTML?
Answer: The id attribute uniquely identifies an element, often used for CSS styling or JavaScript manipulation.

Question: What is the <section> tag?
Answer: The <section> tag groups related content, helping to structure the web page.

Question: What are self-closing tags in HTML?
Answer: Self-closing tags, like <img> or <br>, do not require a closing tag.

Question: What is the purpose of the <main> tag?
Answer: The <main> tag highlights the primary content of a web page, excluding headers, footers, and sidebars.

Question: How do you create a text input field in HTML?
Answer: Use the <input> tag with the type="text" attribute.

Question: What is the <aside> tag used for?
Answer: The <aside> tag defines secondary content, such as sidebars or advertisements.

Question: What is the difference between <b> and <strong>?
Answer: <b> makes text bold for presentation, while <strong> adds semantic emphasis.

Question: How do you embed a video in HTML?
Answer: Use the <video> tag with the src attribute, and include controls for playback.

Question: What is the <header> tag?
Answer: The <header> tag defines introductory content or navigation links at the top of a page or section.

Question: What is the <mark> tag?
Answer: The <mark> tag highlights text, indicating its relevance or importance.

Question: What is the <progress> tag?
Answer: The <progress> tag displays a progress bar, often used to show task completion.

Question: What is the <time> tag?
Answer: The <time> tag defines a specific time or date, often used for timestamps.

6.6 TCP/IP port and URL

Question: What is a common use case for port 22?
Answer: Port 22 is commonly used for Secure Shell (SSH) communication.

Question: What is the use of port 25?
Answer: Port 25 is used for Simple Mail Transfer Protocol (SMTP) to send emails.

Question: What is a custom port?
Answer: A custom port is a non-standard port number assigned to services or applications for specific use cases.

Question: What is the purpose of the Host header in HTTP?
Answer: The Host header specifies the domain name and optional port for the server handling the request.

Question: What is an example of a URL with a port?
Answer: http://localhost:8080/home specifies that the server is running on port 8080.

Question: What is a URL encoder?
Answer: A URL encoder converts special characters in URLs into a format safe for transmission, e.g., converting spaces to %20.

Question: What are well-known ports?
Answer: Well-known ports are standardized port numbers (0–1023) used for widely recognized protocols and services.

Question: How do you test if a port is open on a server?
Answer: Use tools like telnet or nc (netcat) to check if a port is open and accepting connections.

Question: What is the purpose of port 3306?
Answer: Port 3306 is used by MySQL databases for client-server communication.

Question: What is a URL schema?
Answer: The schema is the protocol part of a URL, such as http, https, or ftp.

Question: How does HTTPS differ in handling ports compared to HTTP?
Answer: HTTPS uses port 443 by default, encrypting data using SSL/TLS, while HTTP uses port 80 for unencrypted communication.

Question: What is a URL slug?
Answer: A URL slug is the part of a URL that identifies a specific page, often SEO-friendly, e.g., "blog-post-title."

Question: What happens if two services try to bind to the same port?
Answer: A conflict occurs, and the second service fails to start, as ports cannot be shared by multiple services.

Question: What is the purpose of port 8080?
Answer: Port 8080 is often used as an alternative to port 80 for web servers during development or testing.

Question: What is a canonical URL?
Answer: A canonical URL is the preferred version of a web page URL, used to avoid duplicate content issues in SEO.

Question: How are URL parameters separated?
Answer: URL parameters are separated by an ampersand (&), e.g., ?id=1&name=John.

Question: What is the Connection: keep-alive header?
Answer: It instructs the server to keep the connection open for multiple requests, reducing overhead.

Question: What is the purpose of port 53?
Answer: Port 53 is used by DNS (Domain Name System) for resolving domain names to IP addresses.

Question: How do URLs affect SEO?
Answer: Clean, descriptive URLs improve SEO by making content easier to understand and rank by search engines.

Question: What is the significance of a wildcard port in server configurations?
Answer: A wildcard port listens for connections on all available IP addresses for a specified port number.

6.7 Web Container

Question: How does a web container manage servlet pooling?
Answer: The container maintains a pool of servlet instances to handle multiple requests efficiently.

Question: What are the phases of a JSP lifecycle in a web container?
Answer: Phases include translation, compilation, initialization, execution, and destruction.

Question: What is the role of annotations in servlet configuration?
Answer: Annotations like @WebServlet and @WebFilter allow declarative configurations, eliminating the need for web.xml.

Question: How does a web container handle URL mapping for servlets?

Answer: It maps URL patterns defined in web.xml or annotations to specific servlets.

Question: What is the difference between doGet and doPost in servlets?
Answer: doGet handles read-only requests, while doPost is used for creating or updating data.

Question: What is the significance of the ServletConfig object?
Answer: The ServletConfig object provides configuration parameters for a specific servlet.

Question: What is the default HTTP session timeout in a web container?
Answer: The default session timeout is typically 30 minutes, configurable in web.xml.

Question: How does a web container ensure thread safety in servlets?
Answer: By creating a single servlet instance and using synchronized blocks or methods for shared resources.

Question: What is the purpose of the ServletRequest and ServletResponse interfaces?
Answer: These interfaces enable servlets to access client requests and send responses.

Question: What is an asynchronous servlet?
Answer: An asynchronous servlet allows non-blocking request handling, improving scalability for long-running tasks.

Question: What is the purpose of a deployment descriptor?
Answer: The deployment descriptor (web.xml) configures web application components, mappings, and security.

Question: How does a web container handle resource loading?
Answer: It uses the classpath or resource paths like WEB-INF to locate files for the application.

Question: What is the difference between include and forward in a request dispatcher?
Answer: include adds content to the response, while forward transfers control to another resource.

Question: What is the role of the ServletContextListener?
Answer: It listens to application lifecycle events, such as startup and shutdown.

Question: What is the use of the @MultipartConfig annotation?
Answer: It enables file upload handling for servlets using multipart/form-data encoding.

Question: How do you manage session attributes in a web container?
Answer: Use the HttpSession methods like setAttribute() and getAttribute().

Question: What is the purpose of the ServletOutputStream class?
Answer: It allows servlets to write binary data to the client.

Question: What are context parameters in a web container?
Answer: Context parameters are application-wide configuration settings defined in web.xml.

Question: What is a virtual host in a web container?
Answer: A virtual host allows multiple domains to be hosted on the same server with separate configurations.

Question: How do you configure a filter in a web container?
Answer: Use @WebFilter annotation or define it in the web.xml with a filter mapping.

Online Resources

	Practice Paper	YouTube Video Playlist Link
Link	https://forms.gle/NhbzndzP51BDHdJj9	https://www.youtube.com/playlist?list=PLzlh_31VWEFrYDrcJYl6fw8TfqdUoi_Q4
QR Code		

CHAPTER 7
Web Container and Web Application Project Setup

7.1 Setting up Tomcat Container

Question: What is hot deployment in Tomcat?
Answer: Hot deployment allows deploying or updating applications without restarting the Tomcat server.

Question: What are connectors in Tomcat?
Answer: Connectors handle communication between clients and the server, such as HTTP or AJP connectors.

Question: How do you configure logging in Tomcat?
Answer: Configure logging by editing the logging.properties file in the conf directory.

Question: What is the difference between a context and a host in Tomcat?
Answer: A context represents a single web application, while a host represents a virtual host or domain.

Question: What is the use of the work directory in Tomcat?
Answer: The work directory stores temporary files and compiled JSP files for web applications.

Question: How do you undeploy an application in Tomcat?
Answer: Delete the application directory or WAR file from the webapps directory and restart Tomcat if necessary.

Question: How do you configure a virtual host in Tomcat?
Answer: Add a <Host> element in the server.xml file with a unique name and directory path.

Question: What is the AJP connector in Tomcat?
Answer: The AJP connector enables communication between Tomcat and web servers like Apache HTTP Server.

Question: How do you configure environment variables in Tomcat?
Answer: Set environment variables like JAVA_HOME and CATALINA_HOME in the system settings or startup scripts.

Question: How do you debug issues in Tomcat?
Answer: Use the logs in the logs directory, enable debug logging, or use remote debugging with an IDE.

Question: What is the purpose of the META-INF directory in Tomcat?
Answer: The META-INF directory contains metadata files for applications, such as the context configuration.

Question: How do you configure context parameters in Tomcat?
Answer: Define context parameters in the <Context> element of the context.xml file or web.xml.

Question: What is the use of the temp directory in Tomcat?
Answer: The temp directory is used to store temporary files generated during server operations.

Question: How do you deploy multiple applications in Tomcat?
Answer: Place multiple WAR files or application directories in the webapps directory, each with a unique context path.

Question: How do you configure thread pools in Tomcat?
Answer: Configure thread pools by editing the <Connector> settings in server.xml and specifying parameters like maxThreads.

Question: How do you restart Tomcat?
Answer: Stop Tomcat using shutdown and start it again using startup, or use a single restart command in managed environments.

Question: What is the Catalina base in Tomcat?
Answer: The Catalina base (CATALINA_BASE) refers to the directory structure containing configuration and application files.

Question: How do you secure the Tomcat Manager interface?
Answer: Restrict access by configuring strong credentials in the tomcat-users.xml file and limiting IP access.

Question: What is the purpose of the context.xml file?
Answer: The context.xml file contains configuration for individual web applications, such as data sources and session settings.

Question: How do you set up a data source in Tomcat?
Answer: Configure a data source in the context.xml file under the <Resource> tag, specifying database connection details.

7.2 Creating a Servlets JSP Project in Eclipse

Question: How do you clean and build a web project in Eclipse?
Answer: Use Project > Clean to remove old files and rebuild the project.

Question: How do you include CSS in a JSP file?
Answer: Link a CSS file in the <head> section of the JSP using the <link> tag.

Question: What is the role of annotations in servlets?
Answer: Annotations like @WebServlet eliminate the need for web.xml by defining servlet configurations directly in the code.

Question: How do you set environment variables for a project in Eclipse?
Answer: Go to Run Configurations > Environment, and add or modify variables.

Question: How do you handle session management in a Servlets JSP project?
Answer: Use the HttpSession object to create and manage user sessions.

Question: What is the purpose of the @WebServlet annotation?
Answer: The @WebServlet annotation specifies servlet configurations like name, URL pattern, and load-on-startup.

Question: How do you generate a WAR file in Eclipse?
Answer: Right-click the project, go to Export > WAR file, specify the destination, and complete the export process.

Question: How do you add Java EE libraries to an Eclipse project?
Answer: Use the Java EE Module Dependencies option under the project properties to add required libraries.

Question: How do you integrate JSTL in a JSP project?
Answer: Add the JSTL JARs to the project and use the taglib directive in JSP files.

Question: How do you create a database connection in a Servlets JSP project?
Answer: Use JDBC, add the database driver JAR, and establish a connection using DriverManager.

Question: What is the use of the Deployment Assembly in Eclipse?

Answer: The Deployment Assembly ensures that required libraries and resources are included in the deployment package.

Question: How do you add a new server runtime in Eclipse?
Answer: Go to Preferences > Server > Runtime Environments, and click Add to configure a new server runtime.

Question: How do you handle exceptions in servlets?
Answer: Use try-catch blocks in servlet methods or define error pages in web.xml.

Question: How do you perform a hot deployment in Eclipse?
Answer: Modify the code, save changes, and the Eclipse server automatically redeploys the application.

Question: How do you use Eclipse for debugging servlets?
Answer: Set breakpoints in the servlet code, run the project in debug mode, and use the debugger to step through the code.

Question: How do you add dependencies to a Maven-based web project in Eclipse?
Answer: Add dependencies in the pom.xml file under the <dependencies> section.

Question: What is the Target Runtime in a Dynamic Web Project?
Answer: The Target Runtime specifies the application server runtime environment, such as Tomcat, for deploying the project.

Question: How do you handle multiple projects on the same server in Eclipse?
Answer: Add each project to the server in the Servers view and manage their deployment paths.

Question: How do you integrate a database pool in Eclipse?
Answer: Configure the connection pool in the server's configuration (e.g., context.xml in Tomcat) and reference it in the web project.

Question: How do you export a Servlets JSP project for deployment?
Answer: Use Export > WAR File, select the project, specify the destination, and click Finish.

7.3 Web Application Project Structure

Question: How do you structure a Maven-based web project?
Answer: A Maven-based web project follows a standard layout with src/main/java, src/main/resources, and src/main/webapp.

Question: What is the purpose of the test folder in a Maven project?
Answer: The src/test/java folder stores test classes for unit and integration testing.

Question: What is the pom.xml file in a Maven project?
Answer: The pom.xml file manages dependencies, plugins, and build configurations for a Maven-based web application.

Question: How do you deploy a web application in a server?
Answer: Package the project as a WAR file and deploy it to the server's webapps directory.

Question: What is the build folder in a web application?
Answer: The build folder contains the compiled application and resources, ready for deployment.

Question: Where are configuration files stored in a web project?
Answer: Configuration files are stored in the WEB-INF directory or the src/main/resources folder in a Maven project.

Question: What is the role of the views folder in a web project?
Answer: The views folder typically contains templates or JSP files used for rendering the UI.

Question: How are internationalization files managed in a web project?
Answer: Place message bundle properties files in the resources or src/main/resources folder.

Question: What is the purpose of the .classpath file in Eclipse projects?
Answer: The .classpath file defines the classpath for the project, including source folders and libraries.

Question: What is the .project file in Eclipse projects?
Answer: The .project file contains metadata about the Eclipse project, such as its name and build configurations.

Question: How do you include third-party libraries in a Maven project?
Answer: Add dependencies to the pom.xml file under the <dependencies> section.

Question: What is the temp folder in a web project?
Answer: The temp folder stores temporary files generated during application runtime or deployment.

Question: How are REST endpoints organized in a web project?
Answer: Group REST controllers in dedicated packages like com.example.rest and annotate them with @RestController.

Question: What is the difference between WebContent and WEB-INF?
Answer: WebContent contains public resources accessible via URL, while WEB-INF holds private resources like classes and libraries.

Question: How do you configure database properties in a web project?
Answer: Store database properties in configuration files under WEB-INF or resources.

Question: What is the assets folder in a web project?
Answer: The assets folder stores additional static files like fonts, icons, or media resources.

Question: How do you organize API documentation in a web project?
Answer: Include API documentation in a docs folder or generate it using tools like Swagger.

Question: What is the bin folder in a web project?
Answer: The bin folder contains compiled binary files, often used in IDEs for storing bytecode.

Question: How do you manage application-specific properties?
Answer: Store them in a properties or config file under WEB-INF or the resources directory.

Question: What is the role of the public folder in a web project?
Answer: The public folder contains static resources directly accessible by the client, such as images and CSS.

7.4 Configuring Servlet JSP APIs dependencies

Question: How do you avoid class version mismatches in Servlet API?
Answer: Use the exact version of dependencies recommended by the application server.

Question: How do you include dependencies in a Spring Boot project?
Answer: Spring Boot automatically provides servlet and JSP dependencies when you include the spring-boot-starter-web module.

Question: What is the role of the Servlet API RequestDispatcher?
Answer: RequestDispatcher forwards requests to another resource or includes its content in the response.

Question: What is JSTL?
Answer: JSTL (JavaServer Pages Standard Tag Library) provides reusable tags for common web development tasks.

Question: How do you add Servlet dependencies to IntelliJ IDEA?
Answer: Add the Servlet JAR to the project structure under Libraries.

Question: What are common Maven repositories for Servlet APIs?
Answer: Maven Central and JBoss repositories commonly host servlet API JARs.

Question: How do you use dependency management for large projects?
Answer: Use a parent POM or Gradle multi-project setup to centralize dependency versions.

Question: How do you include dependencies in a WAR file?
Answer: Ensure all required libraries are added to the WEB-INF/lib directory or configured in Maven.

Question: What is the javax.servlet.annotation.WebServlet used for?
Answer: It provides a way to define servlet metadata without using web.xml.

Question: How do you test Servlet and JSP configurations locally?
Answer: Use a lightweight server like Tomcat or Jetty to deploy and run the application.

Question: What is the purpose of the javax.servlet.AsyncContext class?
Answer: It enables asynchronous request handling in servlets.

Question: How do you configure dependencies for JSP compilation in IDEs?
Answer: Add the JSP API library to the build path and enable JSP support in the IDE settings.

Question: What is the role of the javax.servlet.ServletConfig interface?
Answer: It provides initialization parameters for a servlet.

Question: How do you enable Java EE support in Eclipse?
Answer: Install the Eclipse Enterprise Edition or the required plugins for Java EE development.

Question: What is the difference between JSTL and EL?
Answer: JSTL is a tag library for JSP, while EL (Expression Language) is used to evaluate expressions dynamically.

Question: How do you configure Servlet 4.0 dependencies?
Answer: Add javax.servlet:javax.servlet-api:4.0.1 to your build file.

Question: What is the purpose of the javax.servlet.ServletContext interface?
Answer: It provides access to web application-level parameters and resources.

Question: How do you ensure dependency compatibility in multi-module projects?
Answer: Use dependency management in the parent module to centralize versions.

Question: What are Servlet 4.0 features?
Answer: Servlet 4.0 introduces HTTP/2 support, server push, and enhanced async processing.

Question: How do you resolve missing class errors in Servlet or JSP APIs?
Answer: Ensure the correct API dependencies are added to the project, and the classpath is configured correctly.

7.5 Project Structure and Deployment Descriptors

Question: What is the difference between classes and lib in WEB-INF?

Answer: The classes directory holds compiled Java classes, while lib contains external JAR files.

Question: How are static resources handled in a web project?
Answer: Static resources like CSS and JavaScript are placed in the WebContent or src/main/webapp directory.

Question: What is the role of the META-INF directory?
Answer: The META-INF directory contains metadata like MANIFEST.MF and application configuration files.

Question: How do annotations replace web.xml?
Answer: Annotations like @WebServlet, @WebFilter, and @WebListener eliminate the need for explicit XML configurations.

Question: How is a data source configured in web.xml?
Answer: Define a resource reference under the <resource-ref> element in web.xml.

Question: What is the purpose of the welcome-file-list in web.xml?
Answer: It defines the default page loaded when the root URL is accessed.

Question: How do you deploy multiple projects on the same server?
Answer: Place each project's WAR file in the server's webapps directory with unique context paths.

Question: What is a ServletContextListener?
Answer: It listens to application lifecycle events, such as initialization and shutdown.

Question: How do you map servlets to multiple URLs in web.xml?
Answer: Add multiple <url-pattern> elements under a single <servlet-mapping>.

Question: What is the role of the env-entry element in web.xml?
Answer: It defines environment entries accessible to servlets and filters.

Question: How do you deploy a web application with web.xml?
Answer: Package the application as a WAR file, including web.xml, and place it in the server's deployment directory.

Question: How do you configure asynchronous servlets in web.xml?
Answer: Set the async-supported attribute to true in the <servlet> element.

Question: What is the difference between absolute and relative URLs in web applications?
Answer: Absolute URLs include the full path with the protocol, while relative URLs are based on the current context.

Question: How do you secure a web application in web.xml?
Answer: Use <security-constraint> with <auth-constraint> and <user-data-constraint> for role-based access.

Question: How do you handle multipart requests in web.xml?
Answer: Configure servlets with @MultipartConfig or specify a multipart filter.

Question: What is the description element in web.xml?
Answer: It provides a brief description of the web application or components.

Question: How do you deploy a web application with annotations only?
Answer: Use annotations like @WebServlet and package the application as a WAR file without a web.xml.

Question: What is the distributable element in web.xml?
Answer: The distributable element marks the application as suitable for deployment in a distributed environment.

Question: What are the benefits of a structured project layout?
Answer: It improves organization, maintainability, scalability, and ease of deployment.

Question: How do you validate a web.xml file?
Answer: Use XML validation tools or IDE support to check the file against the Servlet API schema.

7.6 Web Application Project Structure

Question: What is the views folder in a web project?
Answer: The views folder typically contains templates or JSP files used for rendering the UI.

Question: How do you organize test files in a web project?
Answer: Place test files in a dedicated folder like src/test/java in a Maven-based project.

Question: What is the role of the logs directory in a project?
Answer: The logs directory stores server and application logs for debugging and monitoring.

Question: What is the use of the temp directory in a web application?
Answer: The temp directory stores temporary files created during runtime.

Question: How is the assets folder used in a web project?
Answer: The assets folder contains additional static resources like fonts, icons, and media files.

Question: How are deployment descriptors defined in Maven projects?
Answer: Deployment descriptors like web.xml are placed under src/main/webapp/WEB-INF.

Question: What is the role of the .classpath file in Eclipse?
Answer: It defines the project's classpath, specifying locations of source files and libraries.

Question: How do you include configuration files in the project structure?
Answer: Store configuration files in the resources folder or under WEB-INF.

Question: How do you manage static resources for web applications?
Answer: Organize CSS, JS, and image files in subfolders under WebContent or webapp.

Question: What is the purpose of the .project file in Eclipse?
Answer: The .project file contains metadata about the Eclipse project, such as its name and build settings.

Question: How are database properties managed in a project?
Answer: Store database properties in configuration files under WEB-INF or the resources folder.

Question: How do you organize controller classes in a web project?
Answer: Place controller classes in a dedicated package like com.example.controllers.

Question: What is the structure of a Gradle-based web project?
Answer: It includes src/main/java, src/main/resources, and src/main/webapp for code, resources, and web content.

Question: What is the pom.xml file used for?
Answer: The pom.xml file manages dependencies, plugins, and build configurations for Maven-based projects.

Question: How are security settings configured in a web project?
Answer: Use the web.xml file or annotations like @RolesAllowed for security configurations.

Question: What is the dist folder in a web project?
Answer: The dist folder contains the packaged application ready for deployment.

Question: How do you organize middleware in a web project?
Answer: Place middleware logic in a separate package, such as com.example.middleware.

Question: What is the purpose of the bin folder in Eclipse projects?
Answer: The bin folder contains compiled .class files for the project.

Question: How do you deploy multiple applications on a single server?
Answer: Use unique context paths for each application in the server's configuration.

Question: How is version control managed for a project structure?
Answer: Use gitignore to exclude unnecessary files and directories, and commit essential files to a Git repository.

Online Resources

	Practice Paper	YouTube Video Playlist Link
Link	https://forms.gle/e1zXHwr3aeCiWf4c9	https://www.youtube.com/playlist?list=PLzlh_31VWEFrXjFY5rN0-s5xYEApWMbVW
QR Code		

CHAPTER 8
Servlets

8.1 Introduction to Servlets

Question: How do you pass parameters to a servlet?
Answer: Use query strings in the URL or form data sent in an HTTP request.

Question: What is the RequestDispatcher in servlets?
Answer: The RequestDispatcher forwards requests to another resource or includes its content in the response.

Question: What is a session in a servlet?
Answer: A session is a way to maintain state between client requests using the HttpSession object.

Question: What are servlet filters?
Answer: Filters are used for preprocessing and postprocessing requests and responses, such as for logging or authentication.

Question: How are cookies managed in servlets?
Answer: Use the Cookie class to create, read, and manage cookies in servlets.

Question: What is a thread-safe servlet?
Answer: A thread-safe servlet synchronizes shared resources to prevent data inconsistency.

Question: How do you handle exceptions in a servlet?
Answer: Use try-catch blocks or define error pages in web.xml for specific exceptions.

Question: What are servlet listeners?
Answer: Listeners monitor servlet events like initialization, destruction, and session creation.

Question: What is the purpose of the ServletOutputStream class?
Answer: It is used to write binary data to the client in the servlet response.

Question: How do you redirect a request in a servlet?
Answer: Use the sendRedirect() method of the HttpServletResponse class.

Question: How do you configure servlet initialization parameters?
Answer: Define them in web.xml using <init-param> or use annotations.

Question: What is a servlet chaining?
Answer: Servlet chaining involves passing a request from one servlet to another using RequestDispatcher.

Question: What are asynchronous servlets?
Answer: Asynchronous servlets handle long-running tasks without blocking the main thread, improving performance.

Question: How does a servlet handle form data?
Answer: Use the getParameter() method of HttpServletRequest to retrieve form field values.

Question: What is the servlet thread model?
Answer: A servlet uses a single instance and handles each request in a separate thread.

Question: What are the common HTTP status codes used in servlets?
Answer: Common codes include 200 (OK), 404 (Not Found), and 500 (Internal Server Error).

Question: How do you configure security in a servlet?
Answer: Use web.xml to define security constraints or annotations like @RolesAllowed.

Question: What is the purpose of the HttpServletRequest interface?
Answer: It provides methods to access request parameters, headers, and attributes.

Question: What is the HttpServletResponse interface?
Answer: It provides methods to set response headers, content type, and status codes.

Question: What is the difference between a forward and a redirect in servlets?
Answer: Forward transfers control within the server, while redirect sends a new request to the client.

8.2 Servlet Code Structure

Question: How do you set HTTP status codes in a response?
Answer: Use response.setStatus(HttpServletResponse.SC_OK) to set the status code.

Question: What is the purpose of the getServletConfig() method?
Answer: It retrieves the ServletConfig object, which holds initialization parameters.

Question: What is the role of the getServletContext() method?
Answer: It retrieves the ServletContext object, providing shared resources and configuration data.

Question: How do you create a servlet configuration parameter?
Answer: Define it in web.xml using <init-param> and access it with getInitParameter().

Question: How do you set a custom header in the servlet response?
Answer: Use response.setHeader("HeaderName", "HeaderValue") to set a custom header.

Question: What is the PrintWriter object in a servlet?
Answer: It writes character data to the response output stream.

Question: How do you handle file downloads in a servlet?
Answer: Set the response content type and headers, and write the file content to the response output stream.

Question: How do you manage session data in a servlet?
Answer: Use HttpSession obtained via request.getSession().

Question: What is the difference between doPut() and doDelete() methods?
Answer: doPut() handles HTTP PUT requests, while doDelete() processes DELETE requests.

Question: How do you handle large data in servlets?
Answer: Use buffered streams like BufferedReader and BufferedWriter for efficient data handling.

Question: How do you specify load-on-startup for a servlet?
Answer: Use the <load-on-startup> element in web.xml to initialize a servlet at startup.

Question: How do you handle exceptions in servlet code?
Answer: Use try-catch blocks or define error pages in web.xml.

Question: How do you define URL patterns for a servlet?
Answer: Use the <url-pattern> tag in web.xml or the urlPatterns attribute of @WebServlet.

Question: What is servlet chaining?
Answer: Servlet chaining involves forwarding a request from one servlet to another.

Question: How do you read request headers in a servlet?
Answer: Use request.getHeader("headerName") to retrieve the value of a request header.

Question: How do you define a servlet using annotations?
Answer: Use the @WebServlet annotation with attributes like name and urlPatterns.

Question: What is the purpose of the getAttribute() method?
Answer: It retrieves attributes stored in the request, session, or application scope.

Question: How do you add cookies in a servlet?
Answer: Use the addCookie() method of the HttpServletResponse object.

Question: How do you handle asynchronous processing in servlets?
Answer: Use AsyncContext to manage asynchronous request processing.

Question: How do you log messages in a servlet?
Answer: Use the log() method of the ServletContext or ServletConfig.

8.3 HTTP Methods

Question: How is the TRACE method secured?
Answer: TRACE is often disabled on servers to prevent cross-site tracing (XST) attacks.

Question: How do you return JSON data in response to a GET request?
Answer: Set the response content type to application/json and write the JSON data using response.getWriter().

Question: What is the purpose of the CONNECT method?
Answer: The CONNECT method establishes a tunnel to the server, commonly used for HTTPS connections.

Question: How do you retrieve headers from an HTTP request?
Answer: Use request.getHeader("headerName") to get header values.

Question: How do you set headers in an HTTP response?
Answer: Use response.setHeader("headerName", "headerValue") to set custom headers.

Question: How do you implement custom error handling for HTTP methods?
Answer: Define error pages in web.xml or use try-catch blocks in the servlet methods.

Question: How do you test different HTTP methods?
Answer: Use tools like Postman, cURL, or browser extensions to send requests with various methods.

Question: How do you restrict HTTP methods in servlets?
Answer: Override only the required methods (e.g., doGet()) and leave others unimplemented.

Question: What is the default behavior of the service() method?
Answer: The service() method delegates requests to appropriate HTTP method handlers like doGet() or doPost().

Question: How do you log HTTP method details in servlets?
Answer: Use log(request.getMethod()) to log the HTTP method used in the request.

Question: What is the maximum length for a URL in a GET request?
Answer: The maximum length depends on the browser and server, typically around 2048 characters.

Question: How do you handle CORS for HTTP methods?

Answer: Add CORS headers (e.g., Access-Control-Allow-Origin) in the servlet response.

Question: What are cacheable HTTP methods?
Answer: Methods like GET and HEAD are cacheable, whereas POST is not.

Question: How do you debug HTTP methods in a servlet?
Answer: Log request details like method, headers, and parameters using the servlet's log() method.

Question: What is the purpose of the HEAD method in servlets?
Answer: The HEAD method retrieves metadata (headers) about a resource without fetching the body.

Question: How do you restrict a servlet to only accept POST requests?
Answer: Implement logic in the service() or doGet() method to reject non-POST requests.

Question: What is the status code for a successful POST request?
Answer: The status code for a successful POST request is 201 (Created) or 200 (OK).

Question: How do you pass parameters in a POST request?
Answer: Parameters are sent in the body of the request, often as form data or JSON.

Question: How do you secure HTTP methods in a servlet?
Answer: Use annotations like @RolesAllowed or configure security constraints in web.xml.

Question: How do you handle PUT requests in a servlet?
Answer: Override the doPut() method and parse the request body to update or create a resource.

8.4 Servlet Lifecycle

Question: What is lazy loading in servlets?
Answer: Lazy loading means the servlet is loaded into memory only when the first request is received.

Question: What is eager loading in servlets?
Answer: Eager loading ensures the servlet is loaded and initialized at server startup, configured using <load-on-startup>.

Question: What is the default behavior of servlet loading?
Answer: By default, servlets are loaded lazily, i.e., only upon receiving the first request.

Question: How do you handle shared resources in servlets?
Answer: Use synchronization to manage access to shared resources in a multithreaded environment.

Question: Can a servlet instance be reused?
Answer: Yes, a single servlet instance can handle multiple requests, improving performance through reuse.

Question: What is the purpose of the ServletConfig object?
Answer: The ServletConfig object provides configuration information specific to a servlet.

Question: What is the purpose of the ServletContext object?
Answer: The ServletContext object provides application-level configuration and shared resources.

Question: Can multiple servlets share the same ServletContext?
Answer: Yes, all servlets within the same web application share a single ServletContext.

Question: How do you perform logging in a servlet?
Answer: Use the log() method of the ServletConfig or ServletContext object to log messages.

Question: Can a servlet be reloaded without restarting the server?
Answer: Yes, depending on the container, changes to servlets can trigger automatic reloading.

Question: What happens if the destroy() method is not overridden?
Answer: The default destroy() implementation does nothing, but resource cleanup may be missed.

Question: Can you override the service() method in a servlet?
Answer: Yes, the service() method can be overridden to handle all request types directly.

Question: What is the role of the servlet container in lifecycle management?
Answer: The servlet container handles loading, initializing, invoking, and destroying servlets.

Question: What are the benefits of lazy loading?
Answer: Lazy loading reduces memory usage and speeds up server startup by loading servlets only when needed.

Question: What are the benefits of eager loading?
Answer: Eager loading ensures critical servlets are initialized and ready to handle requests immediately at server startup.

Question: How does a servlet handle exceptions during initialization?
Answer: Exceptions thrown during init() are propagated to the container, which may log the error and prevent the servlet from loading.

Question: What is the use of the getServletInfo() method?
Answer: It provides information about the servlet, such as its version and author.

Question: How do you ensure thread safety in a servlet?
Answer: Avoid using instance variables or synchronize access to shared resources.

Question: What is servlet pooling?
Answer: Servlet pooling is the reuse of servlet instances by the container to improve performance.

Question: Can a servlet lifecycle be controlled programmatically?
Answer: No, the servlet lifecycle is entirely managed by the servlet container.

8.5 Servlet Context and Servlet Config

Question: What is the lifecycle of ServletConfig?
Answer: ServletConfig is created when the servlet is initialized and destroyed when the servlet is unloaded.

Question: What is the lifecycle of ServletContext?
Answer: ServletContext exists as long as the web application is deployed and running on the server.

Question: How do you set context-wide parameters in web.xml?
Answer: Use the <context-param> element with <param-name> and <param-value> tags.

Question: What is the use of the getContext(String uripath) method?
Answer: It retrieves a ServletContext for a specific URI, typically for cross-context communication.

Question: How do you remove attributes from ServletContext?
Answer: Use the removeAttribute(String name) method.

Question: Can ServletContext attributes be serialized?
Answer: Yes, if the attribute implements the Serializable interface.

Question: How do you share data between servlets using ServletContext?
Answer: Store the data as an attribute in ServletContext and retrieve it in other servlets.

Question: Can multiple servlets have different ServletConfig objects?
Answer: Yes, each servlet has its own ServletConfig.

Question: How do you retrieve the names of all ServletContext attributes?
Answer: Use the getAttributeNames() method to retrieve an Enumeration of attribute names.

Question: What happens if ServletContext attributes conflict?
Answer: The latest setAttribute() call overwrites the existing value.

Question: How do you retrieve the major version of the Servlet API?
Answer: Use the getMajorVersion() method of ServletContext.

Question: How do you retrieve the minor version of the Servlet API?
Answer: Use the getMinorVersion() method of ServletContext.

Question: What is the default encoding for resources retrieved via ServletContext?
Answer: The default encoding is determined by the server but can be explicitly set for each resource.

Question: How do you ensure thread safety with ServletContext attributes?
Answer: Synchronize access to shared attributes when modifying them in a multithreaded environment.

Question: Can you have multiple ServletContext objects in a web application?
Answer: No, there is only one ServletContext per web application.

Question: What is the maximum size for ServletContext attributes?
Answer: There is no predefined limit, but the size is constrained by the server and application memory.

Question: Can ServletConfig be null?
Answer: No, ServletConfig is initialized by the container and is never null for a properly configured servlet.

Question: How do you access ServletContext in a JSP?
Answer: Use the application implicit object to access ServletContext in JSP.

Question: Can ServletContext be serialized?
Answer: No, ServletContext itself is not serializable.

Question: How do you handle null attributes in ServletContext?
Answer: Check for null values before accessing or casting the attribute to avoid runtime exceptions.

8.6 Forwarding and Redirection of Requests

Question: Does redirection change the browser's URL?
Answer: Yes, the URL changes to the new location in the browser.

Question: What is the impact of forwarding on session data?
Answer: Session data remains unchanged as the same request object is passed.

Question: How do you handle exceptions during forwarding?
Answer: Use try-catch blocks to catch exceptions and redirect to an error page if needed.

Question: What happens to HTTP headers during forwarding?
Answer: HTTP headers remain the same during forwarding since the response is not committed.

Question: What happens to HTTP headers during redirection?
Answer: New HTTP headers are sent to the client during redirection.

Question: Can you forward a request multiple times?
Answer: Yes, but it is not a common practice and can lead to complex code.

Question: Can you redirect a request multiple times?
Answer: Yes, but excessive redirection can degrade user experience and performance.

Question: How do you debug forwarding issues?
Answer: Check the server logs and ensure the resource path is correct.

Question: How do you debug redirection issues?
Answer: Verify the URL passed to sendRedirect() and ensure it is accessible.

Question: How do you forward a request to a JSP?
Answer: Use RequestDispatcher and specify the JSP path, e.g., request.getRequestDispatcher("example.jsp").forward(request, response).

Question: Can you include dynamic content using forwarding?
Answer: Yes, forwarding can include servlets, JSPs, or dynamic resources.

Question: How do you redirect a request to a login page?
Answer: Use response.sendRedirect("login.jsp") to redirect to the login page.

Question: What is the purpose of the include() method in forwarding?
Answer: It includes the content of another resource in the response without transferring control.

Question: How do you log forwarding actions in a servlet?
Answer: Use the log() method of ServletContext or ServletConfig to log forwarding details.

Question: How do you handle errors during redirection?
Answer: Catch exceptions and log the error before sending a fallback redirect, e.g., response.sendRedirect("error.jsp").

Question: What is the impact of forwarding on cookies?
Answer: Cookies remain intact during forwarding as the client is unaware of the resource change.

Question: What is the impact of redirection on cookies?
Answer: Redirection may cause the client to resend cookies if the redirected resource is on the same domain.

Question: Can you redirect to a resource on another domain?
Answer: Yes, sendRedirect() can redirect to resources on external domains.

Question: How does redirection handle HTTPS and HTTP?
Answer: Redirection can switch between protocols if the target URL specifies a different protocol.

Question: What is the preferred approach for internal resource calls, forward or redirect?
Answer: Forward is preferred for internal resource calls as it avoids unnecessary client round trips.

Online Resources

	Practice Paper	YouTube Video Playlist Link
Link	https://forms.gle/KCd3wxQJ35RS4MjMA	https://www.youtube.com/playlist?list=PLzlh_31VWEFqc1WrGhl0GA26b13vgs3YK
QR Code		

CHAPTER 9
Session Management

9.1 Understanding Sessions

Question: What is a session fixation attack?
Answer: It is an attack where an attacker tricks a user into using a pre-determined session ID.

Question: How do you prevent session fixation attacks?
Answer: Regenerate the session ID using request.getSession(true) after user login.

Question: Can sessions be shared between applications?
Answer: No, sessions are application-specific and cannot be shared between different web applications.

Question: How do you make a session persistent?
Answer: Use cookies with the HttpOnly and Secure flags for a persistent session, if required.

Question: What is the scope of a session?
Answer: The scope of a session is limited to a single user's interaction with a specific web application.

Question: How do you track sessions in HTTPS?
Answer: HTTPS ensures secure communication, and session tracking is done using secure cookies.

Question: What is the session.getId() method?
Answer: It retrieves the unique session ID associated with the user's session.

Question: Can a session survive a browser restart?
Answer: No, unless a persistent cookie stores the session ID.

Question: What is the maximum size of session data?
Answer: There is no fixed limit, but it is constrained by server memory and configuration.

Question: How do you track sessions without cookies?
Answer: Use URL rewriting or hidden form fields to pass the session ID between client and server.

Question: What is a distributed session?
Answer: A distributed session allows session data to be shared across multiple servers in a clustered environment.

Question: How do you configure session replication in a cluster?
Answer: Use server-specific configurations, such as sticky sessions or database-backed session storage.

Question: What are the common session attributes?
Answer: Session attributes can include user information, preferences, cart details, and authentication tokens.

Question: What is the HttpSessionBindingListener interface?
Answer: It listens to events when attributes are added, removed, or replaced in a session.

Question: How do you log session events?
Answer: Use the HttpSessionListener interface to log creation and destruction of sessions.

Question: Can a session be shared across subdomains?
Answer: Yes, by setting the Domain attribute in the session cookie.

Question: How do you prevent session hijacking?

Answer: Use secure cookies, regenerate session IDs frequently, and enable HTTPS.

Question: What is session affinity?
Answer: Session affinity, or sticky sessions, ensures that requests from a user are always routed to the same server.

Question: What is session persistence?
Answer: Session persistence stores session data in a database or file system to survive server restarts.

Question: How do you manage session timeout for specific users?
Answer: Use session.setMaxInactiveInterval() with a custom value based on the user type or activity.

9.2 Session Information Passing between Client and Server

Question: What is the difference between session cookies and persistent cookies?
Answer: Session cookies exist only for the duration of the browser session, while persistent cookies survive across sessions.

Question: How do you pass session information securely between different domains?
Answer: Use CORS with secure cookies or tokens to pass session information across domains.

Question: What is cross-site request forgery (CSRF)?
Answer: CSRF is an attack where unauthorized commands are sent from a user's browser to a trusted site.

Question: How do you protect against CSRF in session management?
Answer: Use CSRF tokens that must be validated with each request.

Question: What are the limitations of hidden form fields for session management?
Answer: Hidden form fields only work with form submissions and cannot track sessions across multiple pages.

Question: How do you handle session information during a page refresh?
Answer: Sessions are unaffected by page refreshes, as the browser automatically sends the session ID with each request.

Question: How do you restrict session cookies to HTTPS?
Answer: Set the Secure attribute on the cookie to ensure it is sent only over HTTPS.

Question: What is the role of the HttpOnly attribute in session cookies?
Answer: The HttpOnly attribute prevents JavaScript from accessing cookies, reducing the risk of XSS attacks.

Question: Can URL rewriting be used with POST requests?
Answer: Yes, but it is less common; URL rewriting is more often used with GET requests.

Question: How do you handle session expiration on the client side?
Answer: Redirect the user to a login page when the session is detected as expired.

Question: How do you manage session information for multiple tabs in the same browser?
Answer: Session data is shared across tabs in the same browser if they share the same session cookie.

Question: How do you differentiate sessions for multiple users on the same machine?
Answer: Each user has a unique session ID stored in a separate browser session or different browser instances.

Question: How do you pass session information in a clustered environment?
Answer: Use sticky sessions or session replication to share session information across servers.

Question: How do you validate session IDs on the server?

Answer: Validate session IDs by ensuring they match an active session in the server's session store.

Question: Can session cookies work with AJAX requests?
Answer: Yes, session cookies are automatically sent with AJAX requests if the same-origin policy is followed.

Question: How do you handle session information for mobile applications?
Answer: Use tokens (e.g., OAuth tokens) or persistent cookies for session management in mobile apps.

Question: How do you synchronize session information across microservices?
Answer: Use a centralized session store like Redis or pass tokens in headers.

Question: What is the impact of disabling cookies on session management?
Answer: If cookies are disabled, URL rewriting or hidden fields must be used to pass session information.

Question: How do you handle concurrent session information?
Answer: Use session attributes carefully, and synchronize access to shared data when necessary.

Question: How do you log session information for auditing purposes?
Answer: Log session IDs, user actions, and timestamps on the server side while ensuring sensitive data is excluded.

9.3 Session Management Mechanisms: Cookies, Rewriting

Question: How do you handle cookies with different domains?
Answer: Use the setDomain(String domain) method to specify the domain for which the cookie is valid.

Question: How do you restrict cookies to a specific path?
Answer: Use the setPath(String path) method to restrict cookies to specific paths on the server.

Question: What happens if cookies are disabled on the client?
Answer: The server must use URL rewriting or hidden form fields to track sessions.

Question: How do you enable session tracking with URL rewriting in Java?
Answer: Configure the servlet container to use URL rewriting by default or explicitly encode URLs with response.encodeURL().

Question: How do you delete a cookie in Java?
Answer: Set the cookie's value to null and its Max-Age to 0, then add it to the response.

Question: How do secure cookies protect session data?
Answer: Secure cookies are transmitted only over HTTPS, reducing the risk of interception.

Question: Can cookies be shared between subdomains?
Answer: Yes, by setting the Domain attribute to a common parent domain.

Question: How do you handle cookie conflicts in Java?
Answer: Use unique names for cookies and ensure no multiple cookies share the same name and path.

Question: What is the impact of using URL rewriting for session tracking?
Answer: URL rewriting can expose session IDs in browser history and logs, increasing security risks.

Question: How do you detect cookie support on the client?
Answer: Send a test cookie to the client and check if it is returned in the subsequent request.

Question: How do you handle session expiration with cookies?

Answer: Set the session timeout on the server, and the session will expire when it is inactive for the specified time.

Question: How do you enable cookies in a Java web application?
Answer: Ensure cookies are enabled in the browser, and the server sends cookies with response.addCookie().

Question: What are third-party cookies?
Answer: Third-party cookies are set by domains other than the one the user is visiting.

Question: How do you restrict a cookie to the same site?
Answer: Use the SameSite attribute to restrict cookies to the same site or same origin.

Question: How do you manage session persistence across multiple devices?
Answer: Use persistent cookies or tokens stored securely on each device.

Question: How do you handle session IDs in AJAX requests?
Answer: Ensure the browser automatically sends session cookies with AJAX requests.

Question: What is the role of the Cookie class in Java?
Answer: The Cookie class provides methods to create, modify, and manage cookies.

Question: How do you combine cookies and URL rewriting?
Answer: Use cookies by default, and fall back to URL rewriting when cookies are disabled.

Question: How do you test session tracking mechanisms?
Answer: Use tools like Postman, browser developer tools, or cURL to test cookies and URL rewriting.

Question: What are the advantages of URL rewriting?
Answer: URL rewriting does not require client-side support for cookies and can work in environments where cookies are disabled.

9.4 Session Destruction

Question: What are sticky sessions and how do they affect session destruction?
Answer: Sticky sessions bind a user session to a specific server; destruction only affects the session on that server unless replicated.

Question: Can session destruction be triggered asynchronously?
Answer: Yes, use background threads or task schedulers to monitor and invalidate sessions as needed.

Question: How do you ensure that session attributes are removed during destruction?
Answer: Use the HttpSessionBindingListener or manually call removeAttribute() before invalidation.

Question: What is the impact of session destruction on memory?
Answer: It releases memory occupied by session attributes, preventing potential memory leaks.

Question: How do you log session destruction events?
Answer: Implement HttpSessionListener and log events in the sessionDestroyed() method.

Question: How do you destroy all sessions in a web application?
Answer: Use a session registry to track active sessions and call invalidate() on each session.

Question: Can session destruction be scheduled?
Answer: Yes, use schedulers or background tasks to destroy sessions based on specific criteria.

Question: How do you track session destruction across microservices?

Answer: Use a shared session store or event-driven mechanisms to propagate destruction across services.

Question: What happens to session tokens after destruction?
Answer: Session tokens become invalid, requiring clients to reauthenticate to obtain a new session.

Question: How do you destroy a session after detecting a security threat?
Answer: Immediately invalidate the session and clear all sensitive data from memory.

Question: How do you handle concurrent sessions during destruction?
Answer: Use session tracking and selectively invalidate sessions based on business logic.

Question: What is the role of session.removeAttribute() during destruction?
Answer: It allows selective cleanup of session attributes before invalidating the session.

Question: Can you destroy a session without logging out the user?
Answer: No, destroying a session removes all associated data, effectively logging out the user.

Question: How do you destroy sessions in RESTful applications?
Answer: Invalidate session tokens or cookies used for session tracking.

Question: How do you validate if a session is still active before destruction?
Answer: Check if session.isNew() or request.getSession(false) returns null.

Question: What happens to active user sessions during a server shutdown?
Answer: Sessions are destroyed unless persistent storage is configured to save them.

Question: Can session destruction be deferred?
Answer: Yes, by setting a longer timeout or using manual invalidation logic.

Question: How do you destroy sessions across multiple tabs?
Answer: Destroying the session on the server invalidates it for all tabs sharing the same session ID.

Question: What is the role of session listeners in session destruction?
Answer: Session listeners monitor and handle actions when a session is created or destroyed.

Question: How does session destruction affect distributed cache?
Answer: Session destruction triggers cache invalidation, ensuring no stale session data is retained.

9.5 Techniques for Session Destruction

Question: How do you handle session destruction when a user navigates away from the site?
Answer: Rely on session timeout, as navigation events are not tracked by the server.

Question: How do you ensure session destruction after a user closes the browser?
Answer: Use session cookies, which are automatically removed when the browser is closed.

Question: How do you prevent memory leaks during session destruction?
Answer: Ensure all attributes are explicitly removed, and resources like database connections are closed.

Question: Can you destroy a session without invalidating it?
Answer: No, invalidating the session is the standard method to destroy it and release resources.

Question: How do you destroy sessions selectively for specific users?
Answer: Use session tracking and invalidate sessions based on user-specific criteria or events.

Question: What is the impact of session invalidation on cookies?

Answer: Session cookies remain unless explicitly removed; a new session creates a new session ID.

Question: Can a session be destroyed asynchronously?
Answer: Yes, use background tasks or listeners to manage asynchronous session invalidation.

Question: How do you destroy all sessions in a web application?
Answer: Use container-specific APIs or maintain a session registry to track and invalidate all active sessions.

Question: How do you track destroyed sessions?
Answer: Implement the HttpSessionListener interface and log session destruction events.

Question: What is session persistence, and how does it affect destruction?
Answer: Session persistence saves session data between server restarts, requiring explicit removal from the persistent store.

Question: How do you handle session destruction in a cluster?
Answer: Use distributed session management solutions to replicate session invalidation across nodes.

Question: How do you destroy a session in a RESTful application?
Answer: Invalidate the session token or cookie associated with the session.

Question: What is the invalidate() method's behavior on session attributes?
Answer: The invalidate() method removes all session attributes before marking the session as invalid.

Question: How do you destroy expired sessions?
Answer: The servlet container automatically invalidates expired sessions based on the configured timeout.

Question: Can session destruction be reversed?
Answer: No, once a session is invalidated, it cannot be reused or restored.

Question: How do you log out a user across multiple devices?
Answer: Use server-side session tracking and invalidate all sessions associated with the user.

Question: How do you remove sensitive data from memory during session destruction?
Answer: Explicitly clear sensitive attributes and release resources during session invalidation.

Question: How does session destruction improve security?
Answer: Session destruction prevents unauthorized access by removing session data after logout or timeout.

Question: How do you destroy sessions based on inactivity?
Answer: Configure session timeout or track inactivity manually and invalidate the session programmatically.

Question: How do you handle cleanup of external resources during session destruction?
Answer: Use the HttpSessionListener to release external resources like database connections or cached objects.

Online Resources

	Practice Paper	YouTube Video Playlist Link
Link	https://forms.gle/QL58iXQTLuEDL6N96	https://www.youtube.com/playlist?list=PLzlh_31VWEFrqnmvicr5j-5aIQOHLGgb7
QR Code		

CHAPTER 10
Java Server Pages (JSP)

10.1 Introduction to JSP

Question: What are implicit objects in JSP?
Answer: Implicit objects are pre-defined objects available in JSP, such as request, response, session, application, and out.

Question: What is the use of the request implicit object?
Answer: The request object represents the HTTP request sent by the client and provides access to request parameters and attributes.

Question: How do you share data between JSP pages?
Answer: Data can be shared using request attributes, session attributes, or application attributes.

Question: What is a JSP comment?
Answer: A JSP comment <%-- comment --%> is not included in the response sent to the client.

Question: What is a JSP expression language (EL)?
Answer: EL simplifies access to data stored in JavaBeans, arrays, or collections in JSP pages.

Question: How do you disable session tracking in a JSP page?
Answer: Use the <%@ page session="false" %> directive to disable session tracking.

Question: What is the role of the response implicit object in JSP?
Answer: The response object represents the HTTP response sent back to the client and is used to set headers and content.

Question: How do you handle exceptions in JSP?
Answer: Use the <%@ page errorPage="error.jsp" %> directive to specify an error page.

Question: What is the application implicit object in JSP?
Answer: The application object provides a shared scope for the entire web application.

Question: How do you initialize variables in JSP?
Answer: Use scriptlets or declarations to initialize variables in JSP.

Question: What is the advantage of using JSP over PHP?
Answer: JSP integrates seamlessly with Java-based backend systems and provides robust session management and scalability.

Question: How is JSP translated into a Servlet?
Answer: The JSP container converts JSP code into a Servlet class during runtime.

Question: What is the role of the <%@ taglib %> directive in JSP?
Answer: It declares a custom tag library to be used in the JSP page.

Question: What is the use of custom tags in JSP?
Answer: Custom tags extend JSP functionality and simplify complex logic by encapsulating reusable components.

Question: How do you use JavaBeans in JSP?
Answer: Use the jsp:useBean tag to instantiate and access JavaBeans in JSP pages.

Question: How do you specify the scope of a JavaBean in JSP?
Answer: Use the scope attribute in jsp:useBean to set the scope to page, request, session, or application.

Question: How do you configure a JSP page to handle POST requests?
Answer: JSP pages inherently handle both GET and POST requests. To customize, use the request implicit object.

Question: What are the types of JSP tags?
Answer: JSP tags include directives, actions, and scripting elements.

Question: Can JSP pages interact with databases?
Answer: Yes, JSP pages can interact with databases using JDBC within scriptlets or JavaBeans.

Question: How do you optimize JSP performance?
Answer: Use caching, minimize scriptlets, precompile JSP pages, and reuse objects in the appropriate scope.

10.2 Directives in JSP: Page, Include, Taglib

Question: Can <%@ include %> include non-JSP files?
Answer: Yes, it can include HTML or text files as well as JSP files.

Question: What is the isThreadSafe attribute in <%@ page %>?
Answer: The isThreadSafe attribute specifies whether the JSP page is thread-safe, e.g., <%@ page isThreadSafe="false" %>.

Question: How do you declare a page to not use a session in JSP?
Answer: Use <%@ page session="false" %> to declare the page not to use session tracking.

Question: What happens if <%@ include %> includes a file that does not exist?
Answer: The JSP translation will fail with an error.

Question: What is the advantage of using <%@ include %> for headers and footers?
Answer: It ensures consistency and reusability by including static content in multiple pages.

Question: What is the difference between isErrorPage and errorPage in <%@ page %>?
Answer: isErrorPage indicates if the JSP can handle errors, while errorPage specifies the page to redirect errors to.

Question: How does <%@ taglib %> support custom tags?
Answer: It links the JSP page to a tag library descriptor (TLD) file, enabling the use of custom tags.

Question: How do you disable scripting in JSP using directives?
Answer: Use <%@ page scriptingInvalid="true" %> to disable scripting elements in JSP.

Question: What is the use of extends in <%@ page %>?
Answer: The extends attribute specifies a superclass for the generated servlet, e.g., <%@ page extends="MyServlet" %>.

Question: Can <%@ include %> include dynamic content?
Answer: No, <%@ include %> is for static inclusion. Use jsp:include for dynamic content.

Question: How do you handle tag library conflicts in JSP?
Answer: Use unique prefixes in <%@ taglib %> to differentiate between libraries.

Question: Can <%@ taglib %> work with JSTL?
Answer: Yes, <%@ taglib %> is commonly used to include JSTL libraries in JSP.

Question: How does the contentType attribute affect the browser's response?
Answer: It sets the MIME type of the response, affecting how the browser interprets the content.

Question: What is the role of <%@ include %> in modular JSP design?
Answer: It enables reuse of static content like headers, footers, or navigation menus across multiple JSP pages.

Question: How do you manage dependencies using <%@ include %>?
Answer: Centralize shared content in a single file and include it using <%@ include %> for easy updates.

Question: Can <%@ page %> control exception handling in JSP?
Answer: Yes, it specifies error-handling behavior using isErrorPage and errorPage attributes.

Question: How do you reference external tag libraries in JSP?
Answer: Use <%@ taglib uri="path-to-taglib.tld" prefix="customPrefix" %>.

Question: What is the default language for <%@ page %>?
Answer: The default language is Java.

Question: How do directives impact JSP compilation?
Answer: Directives provide instructions during JSP translation, affecting the compiled servlet's behavior.

Question: How do you include CSS or JavaScript files using <%@ include %>?
Answer: Use <%@ include file="styles.css" %> or <%@ include file="script.js" %> to include these files.

10.3 JSP Standard Actions

Question: How do you pass parameters with jsp:param?
Answer: Use <jsp:param name="paramName" value="paramValue"/> inside a parent action tag.

Question: Can jsp:include handle dynamic content?
Answer: Yes, jsp:include dynamically evaluates and includes the response of the target resource.

Question: What happens if jsp:forward is executed after response output?
Answer: It throws an IllegalStateException if response output is already committed.

Question: What is the scope of a bean created with jsp:useBean?
Answer: The scope determines the bean's lifespan and visibility: page, request, session, or application.

Question: What is the default scope for jsp:useBean?
Answer: The default scope is page.

Question: How do you retrieve a JavaBean in the session scope?
Answer: Use <jsp:useBean id="beanName" class="com.example.BeanClass" scope="session"/>.

Question: What happens if a bean does not exist in the specified scope?
Answer: The jsp:useBean action creates a new instance of the bean.

Question: Can jsp:setProperty handle type conversions?
Answer: Yes, it converts request parameter values to the appropriate property types.

Question: What is a use case for jsp:getProperty?
Answer: jsp:getProperty is used to display the value of a bean property in JSP pages.

Question: Can jsp:plugin embed other content types?
Answer: No, jsp:plugin is specific to Java applets or JavaBeans.

Question: How do you handle exceptions in standard actions?
Answer: Use try-catch blocks in the parent Servlet or JSP or configure error handling in web.xml.

Question: How do you use jsp:param with jsp:include?
Answer: Use jsp:param inside jsp:include to pass parameters to the included resource dynamically.

Question: What is the difference between jsp:setProperty and setAttribute?
Answer: jsp:setProperty is specific to JavaBeans, while setAttribute is generic for any object.

Question: Can jsp:forward forward to external resources?
Answer: No, jsp:forward works only within the same web application.

Question: What are the attributes of jsp:plugin?
Answer: Common attributes include type, code, codebase, width, and height.

Question: Can jsp:include call Servlets?
Answer: Yes, jsp:include can include the response from Servlets.

Question: What is the order of execution for standard actions in JSP?
Answer: Standard actions are executed sequentially as they appear in the JSP page.

Question: How do you use nested jsp:useBean actions?
Answer: Nested jsp:useBean actions are not allowed; a single declaration must suffice.

Question: Can jsp:forward preserve request attributes?
Answer: Yes, request attributes are preserved during forwarding.

Question: How do standard actions improve JSP development?
Answer: They encapsulate common tasks, reduce Java code in JSP, and improve readability and maintainability.

10.4 Introduction to Expression Language (EL) and JSTL

Question: How does EL handle arrays and lists?
Answer: EL accesses arrays and lists using index-based notation, e.g., ${array[0]} or ${list[1]}.

Question: What is the <c:remove> tag in JSTL?
Answer: <c:remove> removes a variable from the specified scope.

Question: Can EL handle logical operations?
Answer: Yes, EL supports logical operators like &&, ||, and !.

Question: What is the fmt:formatDate tag in JSTL?
Answer: fmt:formatDate formats dates, e.g., <fmt:formatDate value="${date}" pattern="yyyy-MM-dd"/>.

Question: How does EL access maps?
Answer: EL accesses maps using key-based notation, e.g., ${map['key']}.

Question: How do you import a resource in JSTL?
Answer: Use the <c:import> tag, e.g., <c:import url="header.jsp"/>.

Question: What is the purpose of the fmt:setLocale tag in JSTL?
Answer: fmt:setLocale sets the locale for internationalization and formatting.

Question: How do you check conditions in EL?
Answer: Use relational operators like ${num > 5} or ${name == 'John'}.

Question: Can JSTL work with XML data?
Answer: Yes, JSTL provides XML tags like <x:parse> and <x:forEach> for handling XML data.

Question: How do you localize messages using JSTL?
Answer: Use the fmt:message tag with a resource bundle, e.g., <fmt:message key="greeting"/>.

Question: What are the benefits of using JSTL?
Answer: JSTL simplifies common tasks, reduces Java code in JSP, and improves readability and maintainability.

Question: How do you perform URL encoding in JSTL?
Answer: Use the <c:url> tag, e.g., <c:url value="page.jsp" var="encodedUrl"/>.

Question: What is the var attribute in JSTL tags?
Answer: The var attribute specifies the variable name to store the result, e.g., <c:set var="username" value="John"/>.

Question: How do you pass parameters with <c:url>?
Answer: Use <c:param> within <c:url> to append parameters, e.g., <c:param name="id" value="123"/>.

Question: How does EL handle boolean properties?
Answer: EL accesses boolean properties directly without the get prefix, e.g., ${user.active} for isActive().

Question: What is the purpose of the fmt:bundle tag in JSTL?
Answer: fmt:bundle specifies a resource bundle for localized messages.

Question: How do you use conditional expressions in EL?
Answer: Use the ternary operator, e.g., ${num > 5 ? 'High' : 'Low'}.

Question: What is the <c:redirect> tag in JSTL?
Answer: <c:redirect> redirects the request to another URL.

Question: How do you use EL with custom tags?
Answer: EL expressions can be passed as attributes to custom tags defined in a tag library.

Question: How does EL simplify JSP development?
Answer: EL reduces the need for scriptlets, enabling clean and declarative access to data in JSP pages.

10.5 JSTL (JavaServer Pages Standard Tag Library)

Question: What is the purpose of the sql:query tag?
Answer: sql:query executes a SQL SELECT query and stores the result in a variable.

Question: How do you update data in a database using JSTL?
Answer: Use sql:update to execute INSERT, UPDATE, or DELETE SQL statements.

Question: What is the role of the sql:setDataSource tag?
Answer: sql:setDataSource sets the database connection details for SQL tags.

Question: How do you iterate over SQL query results in JSTL?
Answer: Use <c:forEach> with the result set stored in a variable, e.g., <c:forEach var="row" items="${result.rows}">.

Question: How does JSTL handle XML data?
Answer: Use XML tags like <x:parse> and <x:forEach> for parsing and iterating over XML data.

Question: What is the <x:parse> tag used for?
Answer: <x:parse> parses an XML document into a DOM object.

Question: How do you iterate over XML elements in JSTL?
Answer: Use <x:forEach> to iterate through nodes in a parsed XML document.

Question: Can JSTL handle nested tags?
Answer: Yes, JSTL tags like <c:choose> and fmt:bundle support nested logic and content.

Question: How do you pass parameters in JSTL?
Answer: Use <c:param> within tags like <c:redirect> or <c:import> to pass parameters.

Question: What is the difference between <c:forEach> and <c:forTokens>?
Answer: <c:forEach> iterates over collections, while <c:forTokens> splits a string into tokens and iterates over them.

Question: How do you escape XML characters in JSTL?
Answer: Use <c:out> with the escapeXml attribute set to true.

Question: What is the purpose of the scope attribute in JSTL tags?
Answer: The scope attribute specifies where variables are stored, e.g., page, request, session, or application.

Question: How do you validate data using JSTL?
Answer: Combine JSTL core tags with EL expressions for validation logic.

Question: Can you use multiple JSTL libraries in the same JSP page?
Answer: Yes, you can include multiple tag libraries by declaring them with <%@ taglib %> directives.

Question: How do you set default values in JSTL?
Answer: Use EL with conditional expressions, e.g., ${value != null ? value : 'defaultValue'}.

Question: What is the fmt:parseNumber tag used for?
Answer: fmt:parseNumber parses a string into a number based on locale.

Question: How do you perform string manipulations in JSTL?
Answer: Use EL expressions for operations like concatenation, substring, and length.

Question: What is the purpose of the <c:url> tag in JSTL?
Answer: <c:url> generates URLs with proper encoding and optional parameters.

Question: How do you check if a variable is empty in JSTL?
Answer: Use the empty operator, e.g., <c:if test="${empty variable}">.

Question: What are the benefits of using JSTL?
Answer: JSTL simplifies JSP development by reducing Java code, enhancing readability, and promoting best practices.

Online Resources

	Practice Paper	YouTube Video Playlist Link
Link	https://forms.gle/39U3C5Fwqjo8ebBq7	https://www.youtube.com/playlist?list=PLzlh_31VWEFoytSDG1lrWRVbsPlnvvG3z
QR Code		

CHAPTER 11
Struts Framework (version 2.x)

11.1 Basics of MVC

Question: How does Struts manage session data?
Answer: Struts provides access to session attributes through the ActionContext and SessionMap.

Question: What is the role of the value stack in Struts?
Answer: The value stack stores data used by the View, making it accessible to JSPs through OGNL (Object-Graph Navigation Language).

Question: How does MVC reduce code duplication?
Answer: By separating concerns, MVC allows reusing components like Models and Views across different Controllers.

Question: Can multiple Controllers exist in an MVC application?
Answer: Yes, each Controller handles a specific type of user interaction or module in the application.

Question: How does the Controller decide which View to render in Struts?
Answer: The Controller uses the result configuration in struts.xml to determine the next View.

Question: What is the difference between MVC 1 and MVC 2?
Answer: MVC 1 combines Controller and View logic, while MVC 2 separates them, promoting better design and maintainability.

Question: How does Struts support dependency injection?
Answer: Struts integrates with frameworks like Spring for dependency injection.

Question: What are the main components of the Struts 2 framework?
Answer: Key components include Action classes, Interceptors, struts.xml, Result types, and the Value Stack.

Question: How does MVC improve application testing?
Answer: The separation of concerns in MVC allows testing each component (Model, View, Controller) independently.

Question: What is the purpose of OGNL in Struts?
Answer: OGNL is used for data binding and accessing the value stack in Struts.

Question: How do you integrate MVC with security in web applications?
Answer: Use interceptors or middleware in the Controller layer to validate user roles and permissions.

Question: How does Struts handle user input validation in MVC?
Answer: Struts uses interceptors like ValidationInterceptor and XML configuration files for input validation.

Question: How does Struts manage exceptions in the MVC pattern?
Answer: Struts provides exception handling via interceptors and configuration in struts.xml.

Question: Can the Model in MVC include database logic?
Answer: Yes, the Model can include DAO or ORM components to interact with the database.

Question: What is the benefit of using Tiles with Struts?
Answer: Tiles provide a templating system for consistent layout and design across multiple Views.

Question: How does the View in MVC retrieve data from the Model?

Answer: The Controller populates the value stack with Model data, which the View accesses via OGNL.

Question: What is the purpose of interceptors in MVC?
Answer: Interceptors add cross-cutting concerns like logging, security, and validation to the MVC architecture.

Question: How does MVC enhance scalability in applications?
Answer: By separating concerns, MVC allows independent scaling of the Model, View, and Controller layers.

Question: How do you customize the front controller in Struts?
Answer: Modify the FilterDispatcher configuration in web.xml or extend it for custom behavior.

Question: What is the benefit of using Struts for MVC implementation?
Answer: Struts provides a robust framework with built-in components and features to implement MVC effectively in Java web applications.

11.2 Basic Struts Architecture

Question: What is the use of namespaces in Struts?
Answer: Namespaces group related actions, enabling modularization and avoiding URL conflicts.

Question: How does Struts handle file uploads?
Answer: Struts uses the FileUploadInterceptor for managing file uploads.

Question: What is the purpose of the Validation framework in Struts?
Answer: The Validation framework provides a standardized way to validate user input.

Question: How do you define global results in Struts?
Answer: Define global results in struts.xml under the <global-results> tag.

Question: What is the role of Interceptor stacks in Struts?
Answer: Interceptor stacks are collections of interceptors applied to actions for reusable pre- and post-processing logic.

Question: How does Struts integrate with Spring?
Answer: Struts integrates with Spring for dependency injection, using Spring's BeanFactory or ApplicationContext.

Question: What is the default result type in Struts?
Answer: The default result type is dispatcher.

Question: How does Struts support AJAX?
Answer: Struts integrates with AJAX libraries like jQuery or Dojo for asynchronous updates.

Question: How does Struts handle localization?
Answer: Struts uses resource bundles and i18n interceptors to support internationalization.

Question: What is the purpose of the params interceptor in Struts?
Answer: The params interceptor maps request parameters to Action properties.

Question: Can a single Action return multiple results?
Answer: Yes, a single Action can return multiple results based on conditions defined in struts.xml.

Question: What is a chain result in Struts?
Answer: A chain result invokes another Action after executing the current Action.

Question: What is the purpose of the Prepare interceptor in Struts?

Answer: The Prepare interceptor initializes resources required before executing an Action.

Question: How does Struts manage security?
Answer: Struts uses interceptors and filters to implement security features like authentication and authorization.

Question: What is dynamic method invocation in Struts?
Answer: Dynamic method invocation allows calling specific methods in an Action using URLs.

Question: How are custom interceptors created in Struts?
Answer: Custom interceptors are created by implementing the Interceptor interface.

Question: What is the StrutsPrepareAndExecuteFilter?
Answer: It is the main filter in Struts 2.x, combining the tasks of request preparation and execution.

Question: How do you configure default packages in Struts?
Answer: Default packages are configured in struts.xml using the <package> tag.

Question: What is the role of the Dispatcher in Struts?
Answer: The Dispatcher handles the execution of Action classes and manages the result rendering process.

Question: What is the benefit of using Struts for web development?
Answer: Struts simplifies web development with built-in MVC implementation, powerful interceptors, and flexible configuration.

11.3 Developing a Simple Struts 2 Application

Question: What is the role of Interceptors in a Struts application?
Answer: Interceptors handle cross-cutting concerns like logging, validation, and input preprocessing.

Question: How do you debug a Struts application?
Answer: Use logging frameworks, IDE debuggers, and interceptors for tracing execution flow.

Question: How do you implement internationalization in Struts?
Answer: Configure resource bundles for different locales and use the i18n interceptor.

Question: What is the use of the <constant> tag in struts.xml?
Answer: The <constant> tag defines global constants for the application, such as file upload limits or framework behavior.

Question: How do you test an Action class in isolation?
Answer: Use unit testing frameworks like JUnit to test the business logic in the Action class.

Question: What is the default scope of Action properties in Struts?
Answer: The default scope is the request scope.

Question: How do you define a custom interceptor in Struts?
Answer: Implement the Interceptor interface and configure it in struts.xml.

Question: What is dynamic method invocation in Struts?
Answer: It allows calling specific methods in an Action class by appending the method name to the URL.

Question: Can a single Action handle multiple requests?
Answer: Yes, use dynamic method invocation or parameterized Action classes to handle multiple requests.

Question: How do you deploy a Struts application?
Answer: Package the application into a WAR file and deploy it on a servlet container like Tomcat.

Question: What are the prerequisites for deploying a Struts application?
Answer: Ensure web.xml, struts.xml, necessary JAR files, and application resources are properly configured.

Question: How do you implement session management in Struts?
Answer: Use the session map provided by the ActionContext to store and retrieve session attributes.

Question: What is the role of a JSP tag library in a Struts application?
Answer: Tag libraries like Struts tags simplify rendering data and creating forms in JSP.

Question: Can you use AJAX in a Struts application?
Answer: Yes, integrate Struts with AJAX libraries like jQuery to handle asynchronous requests.

Question: How do you configure global results in Struts?
Answer: Define <global-results> in struts.xml to apply result mappings across all Actions.

Question: How do you specify multiple results for a single Action?
Answer: Use multiple <result> tags within an <action> tag in struts.xml.

Question: How does Struts handle file uploads?
Answer: Use the FileUploadInterceptor to process file uploads.

Question: How do you integrate Struts with a database?
Answer: Use DAO classes or ORM frameworks like Hibernate in the Model layer.

Question: How do you secure a Struts application?
Answer: Use interceptors for authentication and authorization and configure secure HTTPS connections.

Question: What are the benefits of using Struts for a simple web application?
Answer: Struts provides an MVC framework, reusable components, and a flexible configuration system for streamlined development.

11.4 Struts 2 Architecture

Question: How does Struts 2 integrate with Spring?
Answer: Struts 2 integrates with Spring for dependency injection, using plugins and spring-bean configurations.

Question: How does Struts 2 support internationalization (i18n)?
Answer: Internationalization is supported using resource bundles and the i18n Interceptor.

Question: How does Struts 2 support file uploads?
Answer: File uploads are managed using the FileUploadInterceptor, which processes multipart requests.

Question: What is the lifecycle of a Struts 2 Action?
Answer: The lifecycle includes request interception, Action instantiation, Interceptor processing, Action execution, and result rendering.

Question: How are exceptions handled in Struts 2?
Answer: Struts 2 handles exceptions using exception mappings in struts.xml or by implementing custom Interceptors.

Question: How does Struts 2 manage result rendering?
Answer: The result configuration in struts.xml determines how the framework renders Views or redirects requests.

Question: What is the role of the Dispatcher in Struts 2?

Answer: The Dispatcher handles Action execution and coordinates Interceptor and Result processing.

Question: How does Struts 2 handle asynchronous requests?
Answer: Struts 2 integrates with AJAX libraries like jQuery or Dojo for asynchronous updates.

Question: What is the struts.properties file?
Answer: The struts.properties file allows customizing default Struts 2 framework behavior.

Question: How does Struts 2 handle global results?
Answer: Global results are defined in struts.xml under the <global-results> tag for reusable result mappings.

Question: What is the purpose of interceptors in Struts 2?
Answer: Interceptors add cross-cutting concerns like logging, validation, and security to Action processing.

Question: How does Struts 2 support plug-ins?
Answer: Struts 2 supports plugins for extending functionality, such as integrating with Hibernate or Spring.

Question: What is the DefaultInterceptorStack in Struts 2?
Answer: The DefaultInterceptorStack is a pre-defined collection of common Interceptors applied to Actions.

Question: How does Struts 2 ensure loose coupling?
Answer: Struts 2 ensures loose coupling through its configuration-based architecture and use of OGNL for data access.

Question: How does Struts 2 integrate with REST APIs?
Answer: Struts 2 provides plugins and configurations for creating RESTful web services.

Question: What are the advantages of Struts 2 architecture?
Answer: Advantages include modular design, flexibility, support for plugins, and improved productivity.

Question: How does Struts 2 handle AJAX calls?
Answer: AJAX calls are handled using JSON results or integrating with JavaScript libraries.

Question: What is the significance of ActionInvocation in Struts 2?
Answer: ActionInvocation represents the current state of an Action execution, including the Interceptors and Results.

Question: How do you test a Struts 2 application?
Answer: Use unit testing for Actions and Interceptors, and tools like Selenium for end-to-end testing.

Question: What makes Struts 2 architecture scalable?
Answer: Struts 2 architecture is scalable due to its modular design, support for plugins, and separation of concerns.

11.5 Interceptors

Question: What is the modelDriven Interceptor?
Answer: The modelDriven Interceptor pushes a custom object onto the Value Stack, making it the default object for data binding.

Question: How does the scope Interceptor manage scopes in Struts 2?
Answer: The scope Interceptor manages attributes in different scopes like request, session, and application.

Question: What is the purpose of the workflow Interceptor?
Answer: The workflow Interceptor ensures that validation is completed before Action execution.

Question: How do you configure global Interceptors?
Answer: Define them in the <default-interceptor-ref> section in struts.xml.

Question: How do you debug issues with Interceptors?
Answer: Use logging frameworks like Log4j or SLF4J to log details during Interceptor execution.

Question: What is the staticParams Interceptor?
Answer: The staticParams Interceptor sets static parameters in the Action configuration.

Question: How do Interceptors interact with the Value Stack?
Answer: Interceptors can modify or add objects to the Value Stack during request processing.

Question: How does the chaining Interceptor work?
Answer: The chaining Interceptor allows one Action to invoke another Action while preserving the Value Stack.

Question: Can Interceptors alter the execution flow of Actions?
Answer: Yes, Interceptors can prevent Action execution by not calling invocation.invoke().

Question: How does the debugging Interceptor help developers?
Answer: The debugging Interceptor provides detailed logs about the request, response, and Value Stack during development.

Question: How do you handle exceptions in a custom Interceptor?
Answer: Catch exceptions in the intercept method and return an appropriate result or rethrow the exception.

Question: What is the devMode Interceptor?
Answer: The devMode Interceptor displays debugging information when development mode is enabled.

Question: How does the paramsPrepareParams Interceptor work?
Answer: It ensures parameters are set before preparation and again after preparation, ensuring data consistency.

Question: What are custom Interceptor parameters?
Answer: Parameters defined in struts.xml that customize the behavior of specific Interceptors.

Question: How does the profiling Interceptor work?
Answer: The profiling Interceptor logs performance metrics for request processing.

Question: What is the role of the servletConfig Interceptor?
Answer: The servletConfig Interceptor provides access to servlet objects like HttpServletRequest and HttpSession.

Question: How do you write reusable Interceptor logic?
Answer: Implement generic Interceptor logic in a base Interceptor class that can be extended as needed.

Question: What is the sequence of Interceptor execution?
Answer: Interceptors are executed in the order they are listed in the Interceptor Stack configuration.

Question: Can Interceptors modify HTTP headers?
Answer: Yes, Interceptors can modify request and response headers during processing.

Question: What are the advantages of using Interceptors in Struts 2?
Answer: Advantages include modularity, reusability, separation of concerns, and centralized request processing.

11.6 Tag Library in Struts 2

Question: What is the <s:debug> tag used for?

Answer: The <s:debug> tag displays debugging information about the Value Stack on the JSP.

Question: What is the purpose of the <s:textarea> tag?
Answer: The <s:textarea> tag generates an HTML textarea field, binding it to an Action property.

Question: How do you display a file input field in Struts 2?
Answer: Use the <s:file> tag to create a file input field in a form.

Question: What is the <s:radio> tag used for?
Answer: The <s:radio> tag generates a set of radio buttons bound to a property in the Action.

Question: How does the <s:select> tag bind a list to an Action property?
Answer: The list attribute specifies the collection, and the name attribute binds the selected value to an Action property.

Question: What is the role of the <s:password> tag?
Answer: The <s:password> tag generates an HTML password input field.

Question: How do you perform conditional rendering using Struts 2 tags?
Answer: Use <s:if>, <s:elseif>, and <s:else> tags for conditional rendering in JSP.

Question: What is the <s:bean> tag used for?
Answer: The <s:bean> tag creates and initializes a JavaBean and pushes it onto the Value Stack.

Question: How do you iterate over a map in Struts 2?
Answer: Use the <s:iterator> tag and access keys and values using OGNL.

Question: What is the purpose of the <s:checkboxlist> tag?
Answer: The <s:checkboxlist> tag generates a list of checkboxes from a collection.

Question: How do you render a table dynamically using Struts 2?
Answer: Use the <s:iterator> tag to loop through a collection and render table rows dynamically.

Question: What is the <s:push> tag used for?
Answer: The <s:push> tag pushes an object onto the Value Stack, making it the default reference object.

Question: How do you bind multiple values in a form field?
Answer: Use tags like <s:checkboxlist> or <s:select> with the multiple="true" attribute.

Question: How do you format currency in Struts 2?
Answer: Use the <s:property> tag with custom formatting logic or external utilities.

Question: How do you handle dynamic attributes in Struts 2 tags?
Answer: Use OGNL expressions for dynamic attributes in tags like <s:textfield> or <s:submit>.

Question: What is the <s:param> tag used for?
Answer: The <s:param> tag sets parameters for tags like <s:url> or <s:action>.

Question: How do you upload files using Struts 2 tags?
Answer: Use the <s:file> tag and configure the fileUpload Interceptor for processing.

Question: How do you display error messages in Struts 2?
Answer: Use the <s:fielderror> tag to display field-specific error messages.

Question: What is the <s:reset> tag used for?
Answer: The <s:reset> tag generates an HTML reset button in a form.

Question: What are the advantages of using Struts 2 Tag Library?
Answer: It simplifies JSP development, reduces Java code in JSP, and provides a consistent framework for dynamic content rendering.

11.7 Tiles Framework in Struts 2

Question: How do you configure multiple Tiles configuration files?
Answer: Use the <constant> tag in struts.xml to specify multiple tiles.xml files.

Question: How do you test Tiles integration in Struts 2?
Answer: Test Tiles definitions and attribute bindings using mock objects and integration testing tools.

Question: Can Tiles be used with AJAX in Struts 2?
Answer: Yes, Tiles layouts can include dynamic content loaded through AJAX.

Question: How do you render a partial view with Tiles?
Answer: Use the <insertAttribute> tag in JSP to render specific attributes of a Tiles definition.

Question: What is the purpose of the org.apache.tiles.startup.TilesInitializer class?
Answer: This class initializes the Tiles framework during application startup.

Question: How do you override Tiles attributes in a child definition?
Answer: Use the <put-attribute> tag in the child definition to override parent attributes.

Question: What is the advantage of using Tiles over traditional JSP includes?
Answer: Tiles provide a cleaner, more modular approach to layout management compared to static includes.

Question: How do you handle exceptions in Tiles?
Answer: Configure error pages in tiles.xml or use Struts 2 exception handling mechanisms.

Question: How does Tiles manage themes or skins?
Answer: Use different Tiles definitions for each theme and dynamically switch between them.

Question: How do you cache Tiles templates?
Answer: Use server-side caching mechanisms or configure Tiles attributes to improve performance.

Question: How do you log errors in Tiles?
Answer: Use a logging framework like Log4j to log errors during Tiles rendering or initialization.

Question: Can you use Tiles with other frameworks like Spring?
Answer: Yes, Tiles integrates seamlessly with frameworks like Spring MVC and Struts.

Question: What is the role of the <insertDefinition> tag?
Answer: The <insertDefinition> tag inserts one Tiles definition into another.

Question: How do you define placeholders in Tiles?
Answer: Use attributes in the baseTemplate to define placeholders for dynamic content.

Question: How does Tiles manage multiple layouts?
Answer: Use different definitions in tiles.xml for each layout and map them to Actions.

Question: How do you customize Tiles initialization?
Answer: Extend the TilesInitializer class to customize Tiles configuration and initialization.

Question: Can you mix JSP includes with Tiles?

Answer: Yes, JSP includes can be used alongside Tiles for specific use cases.

Question: How do you debug Tiles issues in Struts 2?
Answer: Enable detailed logging for Tiles and inspect the rendered HTML for missing attributes or definitions.

Question: What are common mistakes in Tiles configuration?
Answer: Common mistakes include missing attribute values, incorrect definition inheritance, and misconfigured result types.

Question: Why is Tiles recommended for large-scale applications?
Answer: Tiles simplifies layout management, reduces duplication, and ensures consistency, making it ideal for large applications.

Online Resources

	Practice Paper	YouTube Video Playlist Link
Link	https://forms.gle/ZqG9phCXhVWTS6478	https://www.youtube.com/playlist?list=PLzlh_31VWEFpYOL6QX-brDP98qKT15VMX
QR Code		

CHAPTER 12
Hibernate Framework (version 3.x)

12.1 Introduction to ORM

Question: What is HQL in Hibernate?
Answer: HQL (Hibernate Query Language) is an object-oriented query language similar to SQL but operates on entity objects.

Question: How does ORM simplify complex joins?
Answer: ORM frameworks abstract join operations using mappings and relationships in the entity model.

Question: What is a bidirectional relationship in ORM?
Answer: A bidirectional relationship allows navigation between two related entities in both directions.

Question: What is the significance of the @MappedSuperclass annotation?
Answer: @MappedSuperclass is used to define common properties for multiple entity classes.

Question: How does ORM handle inheritance?
Answer: ORM frameworks support inheritance mapping strategies like single table, joined, and table-per-class.

Question: What is the use of @OneToMany in ORM?
Answer: @OneToMany defines a one-to-many relationship between entities.

Question: How does ORM handle database updates?
Answer: ORM frameworks automatically synchronize entity changes with the database during transactions.

Question: What is a composite key in ORM?
Answer: A composite key is a primary key consisting of multiple columns, mapped using @Embeddable or XML.

Question: What is the SessionFactory in Hibernate?
Answer: The SessionFactory is a factory for sessions and is responsible for managing database connections.

Question: How does ORM handle cascading?
Answer: ORM frameworks use cascading to propagate operations like persist, merge, and delete across related entities.

Question: What is the role of @Transient in ORM?
Answer: The @Transient annotation marks a field as non-persistent, excluding it from database mapping.

Question: How do you define a one-to-one relationship in ORM?
Answer: Use annotations like @OneToOne and @JoinColumn to define a one-to-one relationship.

Question: What are the challenges of using ORM?
Answer: Challenges include managing performance, handling complex queries, and debugging lazy initialization issues.

Question: What is the role of annotations in ORM?
Answer: Annotations simplify mapping configurations, reducing the need for external XML files.

Question: How does ORM handle database vendor independence?
Answer: ORM frameworks use dialects to translate database-agnostic queries into vendor-specific SQL.

Question: What is the Criteria API in Hibernate?

Answer: The Criteria API provides a programmatic way to build dynamic queries in Hibernate.

Question: How does ORM handle batch operations?
Answer: ORM frameworks optimize batch operations by grouping multiple inserts, updates, or deletes into a single transaction.

Question: What is the difference between save() and persist() in Hibernate?
Answer: save() returns the generated ID and persists objects immediately, while persist() does not return the ID and relies on the transaction boundary.

Question: What is the significance of the @Cacheable annotation?
Answer: The @Cacheable annotation marks an entity as cacheable, enabling second-level caching.

Question: How does ORM handle database schema changes?
Answer: ORM frameworks like Hibernate provide tools for schema evolution, such as schema update or migration scripts.

12.2 Introduction to Hibernate 3.x

Question: How does Hibernate manage transactions?
Answer: Hibernate uses the Transaction interface to manage database transactions.

Question: What is the difference between get() and load() in Hibernate?
Answer: get() fetches the object immediately, returning null if not found, while load() uses lazy loading and throws an exception if the object does not exist.

Question: How does Hibernate handle primary keys?
Answer: Hibernate supports primary key generation strategies like AUTO, IDENTITY, SEQUENCE, and TABLE.

Question: What is the use of @Id in Hibernate?
Answer: The @Id annotation marks a field as the primary key of an entity.

Question: What is a Hibernate mapping file?
Answer: A Hibernate mapping file (*.hbm.xml) defines the relationship between Java classes and database tables.

Question: How does Hibernate support caching?
Answer: Hibernate supports first-level (session) and second-level (application-wide) caching to improve performance.

Question: What is first-level caching in Hibernate?
Answer: First-level caching is session-specific and stores objects within the current session.

Question: What is second-level caching in Hibernate?
Answer: Second-level caching is application-wide, shared across sessions, and managed using third-party providers like Ehcache.

Question: What is the Criteria API in Hibernate?
Answer: The Criteria API is a programmatic way to construct and execute dynamic queries.

Question: How does Hibernate handle object relationships?
Answer: Hibernate handles relationships using annotations like @OneToOne, @OneToMany, @ManyToOne, and @ManyToMany.

Question: What is cascading in Hibernate?

Answer: Cascading propagates operations like persist, merge, or delete from a parent entity to its related entities.

Question: How do you map a one-to-many relationship in Hibernate?
Answer: Use the @OneToMany annotation along with @JoinColumn or a join table.

Question: What is a composite key in Hibernate?
Answer: A composite key is a primary key composed of multiple columns, mapped using the @Embeddable annotation.

Question: What is the SessionFactory lifecycle?
Answer: The SessionFactory is created during application startup and closed during application shutdown.

Question: What are named queries in Hibernate?
Answer: Named queries are pre-defined, reusable HQL or SQL queries annotated with @NamedQuery.

Question: How does Hibernate handle batch processing?
Answer: Hibernate optimizes batch processing by grouping multiple inserts, updates, or deletes into a single database transaction.

Question: What is the use of @GeneratedValue in Hibernate?
Answer: The @GeneratedValue annotation specifies the primary key generation strategy for an entity.

Question: How does Hibernate handle schema changes?
Answer: Hibernate provides tools for schema validation and updates, like the hbm2ddl.auto configuration.

Question: What are filters in Hibernate?
Answer: Filters dynamically add query constraints at runtime without modifying the HQL or Criteria query.

Question: What are the main features introduced in Hibernate 3.x?
Answer: Features include JPA annotations, enhanced Criteria API, improved performance, and integration with third-party tools.

12.3 Hibernate Architecture

Question: How does Hibernate architecture handle transactions?
Answer: Transactions are managed using the Transaction interface, which supports commit and rollback operations.

Question: What is the difference between HQL and SQL in Hibernate?
Answer: HQL operates on entities and object properties, while SQL directly works with database tables and columns.

Question: How does Hibernate interact with the database?
Answer: Hibernate interacts with the database using JDBC under the hood, abstracting complexities for developers.

Question: What is the role of the Session in Hibernate caching?
Answer: The Session provides first-level caching, storing entities for the duration of the session.

Question: What is the use of Session.get() in Hibernate?
Answer: Session.get() retrieves an entity from the database and returns null if the entity is not found.

Question: What is the use of Session.load() in Hibernate?
Answer: Session.load() retrieves an entity lazily, throwing an exception if the entity does not exist.

Question: How does Hibernate architecture ensure database independence?

Answer: Hibernate uses dialects to translate HQL and entity operations into database-specific SQL.

Question: What is the ServiceRegistry in Hibernate?
Answer: The ServiceRegistry is responsible for configuring and initializing services required by Hibernate, such as connection providers and dialects.

Question: How does Hibernate architecture handle batch processing?
Answer: Batch processing groups multiple insert/update/delete operations into a single transaction for efficiency.

Question: What is the TransactionManager in Hibernate?
Answer: The TransactionManager coordinates transactions across multiple resources in JTA environments.

Question: What is the use of the Native SQL feature in Hibernate?
Answer: Native SQL allows executing raw SQL queries directly within Hibernate for complex or database-specific operations.

Question: How does Hibernate manage object relationships?
Answer: Hibernate manages object relationships through annotations like @OneToOne, @OneToMany, and mappings in XML.

Question: What is the advantage of using annotations in Hibernate?
Answer: Annotations simplify mapping by embedding metadata directly within entity classes, reducing reliance on XML configurations.

Question: What is the Flush operation in Hibernate?
Answer: Flush synchronizes the session's state with the database by executing pending SQL commands.

Question: What is the role of the Evict method in Hibernate?
Answer: The Evict method removes an entity from the session cache, making it a detached object.

Question: How does Hibernate architecture support multi-tenancy?
Answer: Hibernate supports multi-tenancy through separate schema or database strategies, configurable via the SessionFactory.

Question: What is the ScrollableResult in Hibernate?
Answer: ScrollableResult allows scrolling through query results, useful for handling large datasets efficiently.

Question: How does Hibernate architecture handle schema generation?
Answer: Hibernate can auto-generate or validate schemas using configurations like hbm2ddl.auto.

Question: What is the Second-Level Cache in Hibernate?
Answer: The second-level cache stores entities and collections beyond the session scope, shared across the application.

Question: How does the Interceptor interface work in Hibernate?
Answer: The Interceptor interface allows developers to add custom logic during lifecycle events like save, update, or delete.

12.4 CRUD Operations with Hibernate

Question: How do you perform batch processing in Hibernate?
Answer: Use session-level batching with Session methods or configure the hibernate.jdbc.batch_size property for efficient batch operations.

Question: How do you delete multiple records in Hibernate?

Answer: Use HQL or native SQL queries for bulk delete operations.

Question: What is optimistic locking in Hibernate?
Answer: Optimistic locking uses a version column to prevent concurrent updates from overwriting each other during CRUD operations.

Question: How does Hibernate manage lazy initialization during CRUD operations?
Answer: Lazy initialization defers the loading of related data until explicitly accessed during a CRUD operation.

Question: What is the flush() method in Hibernate?
Answer: The flush() method synchronizes the session's in-memory state with the database.

Question: How do you delete a parent entity with cascading?
Answer: Enable cascading delete using the cascade attribute in annotations or XML mappings.

Question: What is the difference between merge() and saveOrUpdate()?
Answer: merge() works with detached objects, creating a new persistent instance, while saveOrUpdate() reattaches the existing object to the session.

Question: How do you execute native SQL in Hibernate CRUD operations?
Answer: Use the createSQLQuery() method to execute raw SQL queries for CRUD operations.

Question: How does Hibernate handle null values during CRUD operations?
Answer: Hibernate allows null values in entities but enforces database constraints where applicable.

Question: How do you perform a CRUD operation on a Many-to-Many relationship?
Answer: Use a join table with annotations like @ManyToMany and @JoinTable to manage Many-to-Many relationships.

Question: How does the detach() method affect CRUD operations?
Answer: The detach() method removes an object from the session, making it detached and no longer synchronized with the database.

Question: How do you handle concurrent updates in Hibernate?
Answer: Use optimistic locking or pessimistic locking to handle concurrent updates during CRUD operations.

Question: How do you validate entities before performing CRUD operations?
Answer: Use the Hibernate Validator framework to enforce validation constraints on entities.

Question: What is the role of caching in CRUD operations?
Answer: Caching improves CRUD performance by reducing the number of database queries using first-level or second-level cache.

Question: How do you update only selected fields of an entity?
Answer: Use HQL or native SQL to update specific fields directly, bypassing the Hibernate entity lifecycle.

Question: How do you soft delete a record in Hibernate?
Answer: Implement a deleted flag in the entity and filter queries to exclude soft-deleted records.

Question: How do you handle timestamps in CRUD operations?
Answer: Use annotations like @CreationTimestamp and @UpdateTimestamp to automatically manage timestamps.

Question: How do you rollback a failed CRUD transaction?
Answer: Use the Transaction.rollback() method to undo changes when a CRUD operation fails.

Question: How do you update a collection in a one-to-many relationship?
Answer: Update the parent entity, and Hibernate will automatically synchronize the associated collection.

Question: How do you optimize CRUD operations in Hibernate?
Answer: Optimize by using caching, batching, lazy loading, and avoiding unnecessary updates with dirty checking.

12.5 Mapping Collections and Associations

Question: What is the difference between unidirectional and bidirectional associations?
Answer: Unidirectional associations define the relationship in one entity, while bidirectional associations define it in both entities.

Question: How do you map composite keys in associations?
Answer: Use the @EmbeddedId or @IdClass annotations to define composite keys.

Question: How do you fetch associated entities in HQL?
Answer: Use joins in HQL queries, like FROM Parent p JOIN FETCH p.children.

Question: What is the inverse side of a relationship in Hibernate?
Answer: The inverse side is the non-owning side of the relationship, defined using mappedBy.

Question: How do you handle ordering in collections?
Answer: Use the @OrderBy or @OrderColumn annotations to specify the order of elements.

Question: What is the purpose of the @ElementCollection annotation?
Answer: The @ElementCollection annotation maps a collection of basic or embeddable types.

Question: How do you map a List with an index column?
Answer: Use the @OrderColumn annotation to specify the index column for the List.

Question: How do you handle one-to-many relationships with a join table?
Answer: Use @OneToMany with @JoinTable to specify the join table for the relationship.

Question: How does Hibernate handle circular references in associations?
Answer: Hibernate resolves circular references using lazy fetching and the mappedBy attribute.

Question: What is a unidirectional many-to-many mapping?
Answer: A unidirectional many-to-many mapping is defined in one entity without a reference in the other.

Question: How do you map an embeddable collection?
Answer: Use @ElementCollection with @CollectionTable to map a collection of embeddable objects.

Question: What is the difference between @ElementCollection and @OneToMany?
Answer: @ElementCollection is for non-entity collections, while @OneToMany is for entity associations.

Question: How do you define a foreign key in a many-to-one relationship?
Answer: Use the @JoinColumn annotation in the owning entity to specify the foreign key column.

Question: How do you fetch only specific fields in associations?
Answer: Use HQL with selected fields or projections to fetch specific data from associated entities.

Question: How do you configure cascading delete in associations?
Answer: Use CascadeType.REMOVE or CascadeType.ALL in the cascade attribute.

Question: What is the difference between @JoinTable and @JoinColumn?

Answer: @JoinTable defines a join table for many-to-many relationships, while @JoinColumn specifies a foreign key column.

Question: How do you map a Map with composite keys?
Answer: Use @MapKey or @MapKeyColumn along with composite key annotations like @EmbeddedId.

Question: How does Hibernate handle duplicate entries in collections?
Answer: Use a Set collection or unique constraints in the database schema to prevent duplicates.

Question: What is a bag in Hibernate?
Answer: A bag is a collection with no specific ordering or unique constraints, typically represented as a List.

Question: How do you optimize associations in Hibernate?
Answer: Use lazy fetching, batch fetching, and caching to optimize associations in Hibernate.

12.6 Hibernate Annotations

Question: How do you enable cascading with annotations?
Answer: Use the cascade attribute in relationship annotations like @OneToMany(cascade = CascadeType.ALL).

Question: What is the @OrderBy annotation used for?
Answer: The @OrderBy annotation specifies the default ordering for elements in a collection.

Question: How do you define an index column for a collection?
Answer: Use the @OrderColumn annotation to define an index column for List collections.

Question: How do you exclude a field from being serialized?
Answer: Use the @Transient annotation to exclude the field from serialization and persistence.

Question: How do you define a secondary table using annotations?
Answer: Use the @SecondaryTable annotation to map an entity to multiple tables.

Question: What is the @Cache annotation in Hibernate?
Answer: The @Cache annotation enables second-level caching for an entity or collection.

Question: What is the purpose of the @NamedQuery annotation?
Answer: The @NamedQuery annotation defines a static, reusable HQL query.

Question: How do you define multiple @NamedQueries?
Answer: Use the @NamedQueries annotation to group multiple named queries.

Question: How do you handle inheritance using annotations?
Answer: Use annotations like @Inheritance, @DiscriminatorColumn, and @DiscriminatorValue to map inheritance hierarchies.

Question: What is the @DiscriminatorColumn annotation?
Answer: The @DiscriminatorColumn annotation specifies the column used to distinguish entities in a single-table inheritance strategy.

Question: How do you specify optimistic locking using annotations?
Answer: Use the @Version annotation to implement optimistic locking.

Question: What is the use of the @Column(nullable = false) annotation?
Answer: It enforces that a column cannot contain null values in the database.

Question: How do you map a formula in Hibernate?

Answer: Use the @Formula annotation to map derived values calculated from database columns.

Question: What is the @Generated annotation used for?
Answer: The @Generated annotation marks a field as generated by the database.

Question: How do you map read-only properties using annotations?
Answer: Use the @Column(updatable = false, insertable = false) attributes to make a property read-only.

Question: How do you specify fetch types in relationships?
Answer: Use fetch = FetchType.LAZY or fetch = FetchType.EAGER in relationship annotations like @OneToMany.

Question: How do you define a SQL insert order for collections?
Answer: Use the @BatchSize annotation to optimize batch inserts for collections.

Question: How do you define an embeddable type?
Answer: Use the @Embeddable annotation for classes that will be embedded in entities.

Question: What is the @NaturalId annotation in Hibernate?
Answer: The @NaturalId annotation marks a property as a natural identifier, used for uniquely identifying an entity.

Question: How do you define a unique constraint using annotations?
Answer: Use the @Table annotation with the uniqueConstraints attribute to define unique constraints.

12.7 Transitioning from XML to Annotations

Question: How do you define multiple named queries with annotations?
Answer: Use the @NamedQueries annotation, which acts as a container for multiple @NamedQuery annotations.

Question: How do you define cascading using annotations?
Answer: Use the cascade attribute in relationship annotations like @OneToMany(cascade = CascadeType.ALL).

Question: How do you handle lazy fetching with annotations?
Answer: Use the fetch attribute in annotations like @OneToMany(fetch = FetchType.LAZY).

Question: How do you replace XML mappings for secondary tables?
Answer: Use the @SecondaryTable annotation to map entities to additional tables.

Question: What annotation replaces <property name="insert="false" update="false"> in XML?
Answer: Use the @Column(insertable = false, updatable = false) attributes in annotations.

Question: How do you handle enumerations using annotations?
Answer: Use the @Enumerated annotation instead of specifying the enumeration type in XML.

Question: What replaces the <filter> tag in XML?
Answer: The @Filter annotation replaces the <filter> tag for dynamic filtering.

Question: How do you map an embeddable class using annotations?
Answer: Use the @Embedded and @Embeddable annotations instead of the <component> tag in XML.

Question: How do you configure batch size using annotations?
Answer: Use the @BatchSize annotation instead of specifying batch sizes in the XML configuration.

Question: What replaces the <cache> tag in XML?

Answer: The @Cache annotation replaces the <cache> tag for enabling second-level caching.

Question: How do you mark a field as transient using annotations?
Answer: Use the @Transient annotation instead of specifying transient in XML.

Question: What replaces the <natural-id> tag in XML?
Answer: The @NaturalId annotation replaces the <natural-id> tag for unique field identification.

Question: How do you define a formula using annotations?
Answer: Use the @Formula annotation instead of specifying formulas in XML mappings.

Question: How do you define fetch strategies with annotations?
Answer: Use the fetch attribute in annotations like @ManyToOne(fetch = FetchType.EAGER).

Question: How do you map a collection of basic types using annotations?
Answer: Use the @ElementCollection annotation instead of the <element> tag in XML.

Question: How do you handle composite foreign keys using annotations?
Answer: Use @JoinColumns to define composite foreign keys, replacing <key-many-to-one> in XML.

Question: How do you transition <subclass> elements in XML?
Answer: Use @Inheritance(strategy = InheritanceType.SINGLE_TABLE) for single-table inheritance.

Question: How do you specify the catalog or schema using annotations?
Answer: Use the @Table(catalog = "catalog_name", schema = "schema_name") attributes.

Question: What is the difference between XML and annotations in Hibernate?
Answer: XML provides external configuration flexibility, while annotations offer inline, code-level configurations.

Question: What are the challenges in transitioning from XML to annotations?
Answer: Challenges include rewriting mappings, maintaining compatibility, and ensuring that complex configurations are accurately represented.

Online Resources

	Practice Paper	YouTube Video Playlist Link
Link	https://forms.gle/YmxduHMXhcv5u3ft6	https://www.youtube.com/playlist?list=PLzlh_31VWEFqTDh51DnkscBdYCozNemEp
QR Code		

CHAPTER 13
Spring Framework (version 3.x)

13.1 Introduction to Spring and DI

Question: What is the difference between @Autowired and @Resource?
Answer: @Autowired injects by type, while @Resource injects by name or type, offering more flexibility.

Question: What is the role of the ApplicationContext in Spring?
Answer: The ApplicationContext interface provides a central interface for accessing Spring's configuration and managing beans.

Question: How does Spring handle singleton beans?
Answer: Spring creates a single instance of a singleton scoped bean and shares it across the application context.

Question: What is the use of the @PostConstruct and @PreDestroy annotations?
Answer: These annotations define lifecycle callback methods for initialization and destruction of beans.

Question: What is the difference between @Component and @Service?
Answer: Both mark a class as a Spring-managed bean, but @Service indicates a business logic layer component.

Question: What is the @Controller annotation in Spring?
Answer: The @Controller annotation marks a class as a controller in the MVC architecture, handling HTTP requests.

Question: How do you define bean dependencies in Spring?
Answer: Bean dependencies are defined using annotations like @Autowired or explicitly in the @Bean method.

Question: What is the @RestController annotation in Spring?
Answer: The @RestController annotation combines @Controller and @ResponseBody for RESTful web services.

Question: How do you manage external properties in Spring?
Answer: Use the @PropertySource annotation with a .properties file to externalize configuration.

Question: What is Spring's annotation-based AOP?
Answer: Annotation-based AOP uses annotations like @Aspect and @Around to define cross-cutting concerns.

Question: What is the purpose of the @Configuration annotation?
Answer: The @Configuration annotation marks a class as a source of Spring bean definitions.

Question: How does Spring ensure loose coupling?
Answer: Spring achieves loose coupling through DI, AOP, and interfaces, promoting modular and maintainable code.

Question: How do you enable component scanning in Spring?
Answer: Use the @ComponentScan annotation in a @Configuration class to scan for Spring-managed components.

Question: What is the @DependsOn annotation in Spring?
Answer: The @DependsOn annotation specifies that a bean depends on another bean, ensuring initialization order.

Question: How does Spring manage bean lifecycles?

Answer: Spring manages bean lifecycles using initialization and destruction callbacks like @PostConstruct and @PreDestroy.

Question: How do you test DI in Spring applications?
Answer: Use Spring testing annotations like @RunWith(SpringJUnit4ClassRunner.class) and @ContextConfiguration.

Question: How does Spring handle null injection?
Answer: Spring throws a NullPointerException if a mandatory dependency is null; this can be resolved using optional DI.

Question: What is the @Import annotation in Spring?
Answer: The @Import annotation imports configuration classes into the application context.

Question: How does Spring handle prototype beans?
Answer: Spring creates a new instance of a prototype scoped bean each time it is requested.

13.2 Spring MVC

Question: How do you handle file uploads in Spring MVC?
Answer: Use the MultipartFile class along with @RequestParam to handle file uploads.

Question: How do you enable CORS in Spring MVC?
Answer: Use the @CrossOrigin annotation on controllers or configure it globally using a CorsRegistry.

Question: How do you map multiple URLs to a single handler?
Answer: Use the @RequestMapping annotation with multiple values, e.g., @RequestMapping({"/url1", "/url2"}).

Question: What is the @ResponseStatus annotation?
Answer: The @ResponseStatus annotation sets the HTTP status code for a response directly on a handler method.

Question: How does Spring MVC support internationalization?
Answer: Use the LocaleResolver and resource bundles to provide messages based on user locale.

Question: What is the role of the @CookieValue annotation?
Answer: The @CookieValue annotation binds the value of an HTTP cookie to a method parameter.

Question: How do you secure a Spring MVC application?
Answer: Use Spring Security to define access control rules, authentication, and authorization.

Question: How do you configure multipart support in Spring MVC?
Answer: Use MultipartResolver bean configuration for handling multipart requests.

Question: What is the difference between @ModelAttribute and @RequestBody?
Answer: @ModelAttribute binds form data to a model object, while @RequestBody binds the request body to an object.

Question: How does Spring MVC integrate with Thymeleaf?
Answer: Use a ThymeleafViewResolver bean to render views using Thymeleaf templates.

Question: What is the purpose of the @ControllerAdvice annotation?
Answer: The @ControllerAdvice annotation provides centralized exception handling for multiple controllers.

Question: How do you configure Spring MVC for asynchronous request handling?

Answer: Use the @EnableAsync annotation and @Async methods to enable asynchronous processing.

Question: How does Spring MVC support JSON and XML responses?
Answer: Use MappingJackson2HttpMessageConverter for JSON and Jaxb2RootElementHttpMessageConverter for XML.

Question: How do you configure static resource handling in Spring MVC?
Answer: Use @EnableWebMvc with the addResourceHandlers() method to map static resource paths.

Question: What is the @MatrixVariable annotation?
Answer: The @MatrixVariable annotation binds matrix variables in the URI to method parameters.

Question: How do you send custom HTTP status codes in Spring MVC?
Answer: Use the ResponseEntity class or the @ResponseStatus annotation.

Question: How does Spring MVC handle redirection?
Answer: Return a redirect: prefix in the controller method, e.g., return "redirect:/home";.

Question: How do you test Spring MVC controllers?
Answer: Use MockMvc for unit testing controllers without starting a full application context.

Question: What is the FlashAttributes mechanism in Spring MVC?
Answer: FlashAttributes temporarily store attributes in a session to survive a redirect request.

Question: What is the role of the HandlerInterceptor in Spring MVC?
Answer: The HandlerInterceptor interface allows pre- and post-processing of HTTP requests in Spring MVC.

13.3 Spring AOP

Question: How do you apply AOP to specific methods?
Answer: Use pointcut expressions to match specific methods for applying advice.

Question: What is the default scope of an aspect in Spring AOP?
Answer: The default scope of an aspect is singleton, meaning a single instance of the aspect is shared across the application.

Question: What is a weaving process in AOP?
Answer: Weaving is the process of linking aspects with target objects, which can occur at compile time, load time, or runtime.

Question: How do you exclude methods from AOP?
Answer: Use a pointcut expression with negation (!execution(...)) to exclude specific methods.

Question: What are some real-world use cases of Spring AOP?
Answer: Common use cases include logging, security checks, transaction management, and performance monitoring.

Question: What is the order of advice execution in Spring AOP?
Answer: The order depends on the advice type: @Before, @Around, @AfterReturning, @AfterThrowing, and finally @After.

Question: How does @Order annotation work in Spring AOP?
Answer: The @Order annotation specifies the execution precedence of aspects, with lower values indicating higher priority.

Question: Can an aspect apply to multiple classes?

Answer: Yes, aspects can be applied to multiple classes using pointcut expressions that match a package or naming pattern.

Question: How does Spring AOP handle exception handling in advice?
Answer: Use @AfterThrowing to handle exceptions, or catch exceptions manually in @Around advice.

Question: What is the use of proceed() in @Around advice?
Answer: The proceed() method allows the execution of the target method and captures its return value.

Question: What is a join point signature in Spring AOP?
Answer: A join point signature provides metadata about the matched method, including its name and parameters.

Question: Can you use AOP with private methods in Spring?
Answer: No, Spring AOP operates only on public methods due to proxy-based implementation.

Question: How does Spring AOP manage stateful aspects?
Answer: Stateful aspects can use instance variables, but the default singleton scope may require synchronized access.

Question: What is the role of the ProceedingJoinPoint?
Answer: ProceedingJoinPoint is used in @Around advice to access method details and control execution flow.

Question: How do you debug Spring AOP configurations?
Answer: Enable logging for org.springframework.aop and inspect proxy creation and method interception.

Question: How does Spring AOP handle thread safety?
Answer: Aspects with singleton scope need explicit synchronization for stateful operations; otherwise, use prototype scope.

Question: Can Spring AOP be used for transactions?
Answer: Yes, Spring AOP is commonly used to manage transactions declaratively using @Transactional.

Question: How do you test aspects in Spring?
Answer: Use unit testing frameworks with mocked join points or integration tests to validate aspect behavior.

Question: What is the limitation of Spring AOP?
Answer: Spring AOP only supports method-level interception and does not support field-level or constructor interception.

Question: How do you disable AOP in Spring?
Answer: Remove @EnableAspectJAutoProxy or exclude aspect classes from component scanning.

13.4 Setting up Spring Project and Configuring Dependencies

Question: What is the role of the @PropertySource annotation?
Answer: The @PropertySource annotation imports properties from an external file into the Spring application context.

Question: How do you add database connectivity in a Spring project?
Answer: Include dependencies like spring-jdbc or spring-data-jpa and configure database properties in application.properties.

Question: What is the use of the spring-web dependency?
Answer: The spring-web module provides features for building web applications, including RESTful APIs.

Question: How do you configure Spring security in a project?
Answer: Add the spring-security dependency and configure security settings using @EnableWebSecurity.

Question: How do you add REST support in a Spring project?
Answer: Include the spring-web or spring-boot-starter-web dependency and use annotations like @RestController and @RequestMapping.

Question: How do you configure dependency injection in a Spring project?
Answer: Use annotations like @Autowired, @Qualifier, and @Primary for dependency injection.

Question: What is the purpose of the spring-tx dependency?
Answer: The spring-tx module provides support for programmatic and declarative transaction management.

Question: How do you add messaging capabilities in Spring?
Answer: Include the spring-messaging dependency and configure beans like MessageChannel and MessageHandler.

Question: How do you configure file uploads in Spring?
Answer: Add dependencies like Apache Commons FileUpload and configure a MultipartResolver bean.

Question: How do you set up internationalization in Spring?
Answer: Use the ResourceBundleMessageSource bean and configure locale-specific resource bundles.

Question: How do you add caching support in Spring?
Answer: Add the spring-cache dependency and annotate methods with @Cacheable or @CacheEvict.

Question: How do you configure custom beans in Spring?
Answer: Define custom beans in a configuration class using the @Bean annotation.

Question: How do you integrate Thymeleaf with a Spring project?
Answer: Add the Thymeleaf dependency and configure a ThymeleafViewResolver bean.

Question: What is the use of the spring-test dependency?
Answer: The spring-test module provides support for testing Spring components using JUnit or TestNG.

Question: How do you manage external dependencies in a Spring project?
Answer: Use a build tool like Maven or Gradle to manage dependencies in the pom.xml or build.gradle.

Question: What is the purpose of the @Import annotation?
Answer: The @Import annotation allows importing configuration classes into the Spring application context.

Question: How do you enable asynchronous processing in Spring?
Answer: Add the spring-context dependency and annotate the configuration class with @EnableAsync.

Question: How do you configure a Spring Boot application to run on a custom port?
Answer: Set the server.port property in the application.properties file.

Question: How do you configure data validation in Spring?
Answer: Add the hibernate-validator dependency and use annotations like @Valid and @Size in the entity classes.

Question: How do you create a custom annotation in Spring?
Answer: Define a new annotation with @Target and @Retention meta-annotations, and use it with AOP or configuration classes.

Online Resources

	Practice Paper	**YouTube Video Playlist Link**
Link	https://forms.gle/zAM6PsYA23s2GdQ78	https://www.youtube.com/playlist?list=PLzlh_31VWEFrvrBakYUPoVKhin4X9vhG2
QR Code		

CHAPTER 14
Spring Boot Framework (Version 2.x)

14.1 Introduction to Spring Boot

Question: How do you integrate Spring Boot with databases?
Answer: Add spring-boot-starter-data-jpa or spring-boot-starter-jdbc and configure database properties.

Question: What is the default JSON parser in Spring Boot?
Answer: The default JSON parser is Jackson, used for serialization and deserialization of objects.

Question: How does Spring Boot simplify dependency management?
Answer: Spring Boot provides managed dependency versions through the spring-boot-starter-parent or spring-boot-dependencies.

Question: What is the purpose of the @RestController annotation in Spring Boot?
Answer: It simplifies REST API development by combining @Controller and @ResponseBody.

Question: How do you deploy a Spring Boot application as a JAR file?
Answer: Build the project using Maven or Gradle and run the generated JAR with the java -jar command.

Question: How do you enable CORS in Spring Boot?
Answer: Use the @CrossOrigin annotation or configure CorsRegistry in a WebMvcConfigurer bean.

Question: What is the default context path in Spring Boot?
Answer: The default context path is /. You can change it by setting server.servlet.context-path.

Question: How do you enable scheduling in Spring Boot?
Answer: Add @EnableScheduling to a configuration class and annotate methods with @Scheduled.

Question: How do you externalize configuration in Spring Boot?
Answer: Use properties or YAML files, command-line arguments, or environment variables.

Question: How do you integrate Spring Boot with Thymeleaf?
Answer: Add the spring-boot-starter-thymeleaf dependency and place templates in the src/main/resources/templates folder.

Question: How do you implement exception handling in Spring Boot?
Answer: Use @ControllerAdvice and @ExceptionHandler annotations to manage exceptions globally or per controller.

Question: What is the default build tool for Spring Boot?
Answer: Maven is commonly used, but Gradle is also supported.

Question: How do you create a custom starter in Spring Boot?
Answer: Create a library module with the necessary dependencies and configurations, then package it as a starter.

Question: How does Spring Boot support testing?
Answer: Spring Boot supports testing with spring-boot-starter-test, which includes JUnit, Mockito, and Spring TestContext.

Question: How do you enable RESTful APIs in Spring Boot?
Answer: Add spring-boot-starter-web and use annotations like @RestController and @RequestMapping.

Question: How do you enable SSL in a Spring Boot application?
Answer: Configure the SSL properties in application.properties and provide the keystore file.

Question: What is the purpose of SpringApplication.run()?
Answer: It bootstraps the application, starting the Spring context and embedded server.

Question: How do you profile environments in Spring Boot?
Answer: Use the spring.profiles.active property to activate specific configuration profiles.

Question: How do you monitor a Spring Boot application?
Answer: Use Actuator endpoints, integrate with monitoring tools like Prometheus or New Relic, and expose metrics.

Question: What is the role of CommandLineRunner in Spring Boot?
Answer: CommandLineRunner executes code after the Spring Boot application has started, useful for initialization tasks.

14.2 Creating and Deploying Spring Boot Projects

Question: What is the role of the CommandLineRunner interface in deployment?
Answer: It executes code at application startup, useful for initialization tasks.

Question: How do you configure logging in Spring Boot?
Answer: Customize logging levels and formats in application.properties or provide a custom logback.xml file.

Question: How do you set up a database connection in Spring Boot?
Answer: Add database dependencies like spring-boot-starter-data-jpa and configure connection properties.

Question: How do you expose application metrics in Spring Boot?
Answer: Use the Actuator's /actuator/metrics endpoint and integrate it with monitoring tools.

Question: How do you integrate Thymeleaf into a Spring Boot project?
Answer: Add the spring-boot-starter-thymeleaf dependency and place templates in src/main/resources/templates.

Question: How do you handle application shutdown in Spring Boot?
Answer: Use the @PreDestroy annotation or implement the DisposableBean interface to release resources.

Question: How do you deploy a Spring Boot application in Docker?
Answer: Create a Dockerfile, build a Docker image, and deploy it using Docker commands.

Question: What is the purpose of the @EnableAutoConfiguration annotation?
Answer: It enables Spring Boot to configure beans automatically based on the classpath.

Question: How do you set up security in a deployed Spring Boot application?
Answer: Add the spring-boot-starter-security dependency and configure authentication and authorization.

Question: How do you handle application scaling in Spring Boot?
Answer: Deploy the application on cloud platforms with auto-scaling features or use container orchestration tools like Kubernetes.

Question: How do you test a Spring Boot application before deployment?
Answer: Use spring-boot-starter-test for unit and integration testing.

Question: How do you deploy a Spring Boot application to AWS Elastic Beanstalk?
Answer: Package the application as a JAR or WAR, create an environment in Elastic Beanstalk, and upload the package.

Question: How do you debug a deployed Spring Boot application?
Answer: Use logging, remote debugging tools, or Actuator endpoints for diagnostics.

Question: How do you configure health checks for deployment?
Answer: Use the Actuator's /actuator/health endpoint for readiness and liveness checks.

Question: How do you enable hot-reloading in Spring Boot?
Answer: Add the spring-boot-devtools dependency to enable live reload during development.

Question: How do you optimize a Spring Boot application for production?
Answer: Disable devtools, enable caching, optimize logging, and use a profiling system like Spring profiles.

Question: How do you schedule tasks in a deployed Spring Boot application?
Answer: Use the @EnableScheduling annotation and @Scheduled methods.

Question: How do you externalize application secrets in Spring Boot?
Answer: Use environment variables, external configuration files, or secret management tools.

Question: How do you configure a custom server in Spring Boot?
Answer: Add server-specific configurations in the application.properties file or programmatically using EmbeddedServletContainerCustomizer.

Question: How do you deploy a Spring Boot application on Kubernetes?
Answer: Package the application in a Docker image, create Kubernetes deployment and service YAML files, and deploy them to a cluster.

14.3 Spring Boot AOP and Database Integration

Question: How do you handle database migrations in Spring Boot?
Answer: Use tools like Flyway or Liquibase to manage database schema changes.

Question: How do you optimize database performance in Spring Boot?
Answer: Use connection pooling, caching, and indexed queries to enhance performance.

Question: What is the default connection pool used by Spring Boot?
Answer: Spring Boot uses HikariCP as the default connection pool.

Question: How do you configure Hibernate properties in Spring Boot?
Answer: Set Hibernate-specific properties in application.properties, such as spring.jpa.hibernate.ddl-auto.

Question: What is the purpose of @JoinColumn in Spring Boot?
Answer: The @JoinColumn annotation defines the foreign key column in a database relationship.

Question: How do you implement a one-to-many relationship in Spring Boot?
Answer: Use @OneToMany on the parent entity and @ManyToOne on the child entity.

Question: What is the EntityManager in Spring Boot?
Answer: The EntityManager is an interface for managing entity lifecycle and executing database operations.

Question: What is the difference between Session and EntityManager?

Answer: Session is a Hibernate-specific interface, while EntityManager is a JPA-standard interface.

Question: How do you log SQL queries in Spring Boot?
Answer: Enable SQL logging by setting spring.jpa.show-sql=true in application.properties.

Question: What is Lazy vs. Eager fetching in JPA?
Answer: Lazy fetching loads data on demand, while eager fetching loads related entities immediately.

Question: How do you handle lazy initialization exceptions?
Answer: Use @Transactional to ensure the persistence context is active during lazy loading.

Question: How do you enable auditing in Spring Boot?
Answer: Use the @EnableJpaAuditing annotation and annotate entity fields with @CreatedDate or @LastModifiedDate.

Question: How do you handle pagination in Spring Boot?
Answer: Use the Pageable interface and methods provided by JpaRepository.

Question: What is the use of @Query annotation in Spring Boot?
Answer: The @Query annotation defines custom queries in repository interfaces.

Question: How do you configure a secondary data source in Spring Boot?
Answer: Define multiple DataSource beans and configure them in the application properties file.

Question: What is the purpose of the @NamedQuery annotation?
Answer: The @NamedQuery annotation defines pre-written queries associated with an entity.

Question: How do you test database integration in Spring Boot?
Answer: Use the @DataJpaTest annotation for testing JPA repositories and database configurations.

Question: What is the role of caching in database integration?
Answer: Caching reduces database access by storing frequently used data in memory.

Question: How do you secure database credentials in Spring Boot?
Answer: Use environment variables or secret management tools to store sensitive information.

Question: How do you integrate Spring AOP with database transactions?
Answer: Use AOP to log, monitor, or manage transactions, combining @Transactional with advice annotations.

14.4 Database Integration in Spring Boot

Question: What is the purpose of the EntityManager in JPA?
Answer: The EntityManager provides an API for managing the lifecycle of entities and executing database operations.

Question: How do you configure multiple data sources in Spring Boot?
Answer: Define multiple DataSource beans and configure them in the application properties file or Java config.

Question: What is the use of @NamedQuery in JPA?
Answer: The @NamedQuery annotation defines reusable queries associated with an entity.

Question: How do you implement auditing in Spring Boot JPA?

Answer: Use @EnableJpaAuditing and annotate entity fields with @CreatedDate, @LastModifiedDate, or similar.

Question: How do you enable caching for database queries?
Answer: Use Spring Cache annotations like @Cacheable and configure a caching provider such as Ehcache.

Question: How do you test database integration in Spring Boot?
Answer: Use the @DataJpaTest annotation for testing repository methods with an in-memory database.

Question: How do you handle database exceptions in Spring Boot?
Answer: Catch exceptions like DataIntegrityViolationException and SQLGrammarException in a global exception handler.

Question: What is the difference between Session and EntityManager?
Answer: Session is Hibernate-specific, while EntityManager is a JPA-standard interface for persistence.

Question: What is a DTO in Spring Boot database integration?
Answer: A Data Transfer Object (DTO) is used to transfer data between layers without exposing entity classes.

Question: How do you integrate Spring Boot with MongoDB?
Answer: Use the spring-boot-starter-data-mongodb dependency and configure MongoDB properties.

Question: How do you perform batch processing in Spring Boot JPA?
Answer: Use Hibernate's batch processing features by configuring hibernate.jdbc.batch_size in application.properties.

Question: How do you log database queries in Spring Boot?
Answer: Enable SQL logging using spring.jpa.show-sql=true or configure a custom logging framework.

Question: How do you secure database credentials in Spring Boot?
Answer: Use environment variables, encrypted property files, or secret management tools to secure credentials.

Question: What is optimistic locking in JPA?
Answer: Optimistic locking ensures data integrity by using versioning fields annotated with @Version.

Question: How do you perform native SQL queries in Spring Boot?
Answer: Use the @Query annotation with native SQL queries or the EntityManager.createNativeQuery() method.

Question: How do you configure Flyway in Spring Boot?
Answer: Add the flyway-core dependency and place migration scripts in the db/migration folder.

Question: How do you map composite keys in JPA?
Answer: Use the @EmbeddedId or @IdClass annotation to map composite keys.

Question: How do you execute stored procedures in Spring Boot?
Answer: Use the @NamedStoredProcedureQuery annotation or EntityManager.createStoredProcedureQuery().

Question: How do you handle transactions in Spring Boot?
Answer: Use the @Transactional annotation for methods or classes where transactions are required.

Question: What is the role of connection pooling in database integration?

Answer: Connection pooling optimizes database connections by reusing them, reducing the overhead of creating new connections.

14.5 Spring Boot View and Caching

Question: How do you customize the cache key in Spring Boot?
Answer: Use the key attribute in @Cacheable to define a custom cache key.

Question: What is the role of Ehcache in Spring Boot?
Answer: Ehcache is a popular caching provider for managing in-memory and disk-based caches.

Question: How do you enable JSP views in Spring Boot?
Answer: Add a servlet container dependency like Tomcat or Jetty and place JSP files in the src/main/webapp folder.

Question: What is the purpose of the spring.thymeleaf.cache property?
Answer: It enables or disables caching for Thymeleaf templates in production or development.

Question: How do you clear a specific cache entry programmatically?
Answer: Use the CacheManager bean to retrieve the cache and call the evict() method.

Question: What is the @CacheConfig annotation?
Answer: It specifies default cache settings for a class, such as cache names and configurations.

Question: How do you integrate Spring Boot caching with JPA?
Answer: Use JPA's second-level caching feature with providers like Ehcache or Hibernate Cache.

Question: How do you enable response caching in Spring Boot?
Answer: Add HTTP caching headers like Cache-Control or use the @Cacheable annotation for REST controllers.

Question: What is the difference between disk and in-memory caching?
Answer: In-memory caching stores data in RAM for fast access, while disk caching stores data persistently on disk.

Question: How do you handle stale data in a cache?
Answer: Use expiration policies, versioning, or manual cache invalidation to manage stale data.

Question: How do you configure multiple cache names in Spring Boot?
Answer: Define multiple cache names in @Cacheable or in the cache provider's configuration.

Question: What is Caffeine cache?
Answer: Caffeine is a high-performance, in-memory caching library supported by Spring Boot.

Question: How do you test caching behavior in Spring Boot?
Answer: Write unit tests using mock data and verify cache interactions with tools like Mockito.

Question: What is content negotiation in Spring Boot views?
Answer: Content negotiation selects the appropriate response format (e.g., JSON, XML, HTML) based on client preferences.

Question: How do you set up dynamic views in Spring Boot?
Answer: Use template engines like Thymeleaf or FreeMarker to generate views dynamically with data.

Question: What is the role of the spring.resources.cache property?
Answer: It configures caching for static resources, like CSS and JS files.

Question: How do you disable caching in Spring Boot?
Answer: Set caching-related properties to false or remove caching configurations.

Question: How do you handle large datasets in caching?
Answer: Use a distributed cache like Redis or partition data across multiple cache nodes.

Question: How do you use Spring Boot Actuator to monitor cache usage?
Answer: Enable Actuator and access the /actuator/caches endpoint to view cache metrics.

Question: What is the benefit of caching in a Spring Boot application?
Answer: Caching improves performance by reducing database load and speeding up data retrieval.

14.6 Caching in Spring Boot

Question: How do you enable distributed caching in Spring Boot?
Answer: Use caching providers like Redis or Hazelcast to share cached data across multiple nodes.

Question: How do you configure in-memory caching in Spring Boot?
Answer: Use the default ConcurrentMapCacheManager or configure a custom in-memory cache provider.

Question: What is the difference between synchronous and asynchronous caching?
Answer: Synchronous caching performs cache operations in the main thread, while asynchronous caching uses separate threads.

Question: How do you handle cache misses in Spring Boot?
Answer: Define fallback logic in methods to fetch data from the original source when the cache is empty.

Question: What is Caffeine Cache?
Answer: Caffeine is a high-performance in-memory caching library supported by Spring Boot for efficient caching.

Question: How do you enable Caffeine caching in Spring Boot?
Answer: Add the caffeine dependency and configure it as the cache manager in the application.

Question: How do you implement versioning in cached data?
Answer: Use a version number as part of the cache key to differentiate between versions of cached data.

Question: What is the difference between local and distributed caching?
Answer: Local caching stores data in a single node, while distributed caching shares data across multiple nodes.

Question: How do you avoid stale data in a cache?
Answer: Use expiration policies, versioning, or @CacheEvict to ensure the cache is updated with fresh data.

Question: How do you configure multiple cache names in Spring Boot?
Answer: Specify cache names in annotations like @Cacheable or in the caching provider's configuration.

Question: How do you log cache hits and misses in Spring Boot?
Answer: Use a custom CacheManager implementation or integrate with monitoring tools to track cache usage.

Question: How do you test caching in Spring Boot?
Answer: Write unit tests using mock data and verify caching behavior with tools like Mockito or custom assertions.

Question: How do you enable cache preloading?
Answer: Populate the cache at application startup using a CommandLineRunner or custom initialization logic.

Question: What is the CacheAspectSupport class in Spring Boot?
Answer: It is an internal Spring class that provides support for caching-related annotations and operations.

Question: How do you configure hierarchical caching in Spring Boot?
Answer: Use caching providers that support hierarchical caching, like Ehcache or Hazelcast, and configure tiers.

Question: What is write-through caching?
Answer: Write-through caching updates both the cache and the underlying data source simultaneously.

Question: How do you configure cache invalidation policies?
Answer: Use @CacheEvict or provider-specific TTL settings to invalidate cache entries automatically.

Question: How do you optimize cache size in Spring Boot?
Answer: Configure maximum size or eviction policies in the caching provider's settings.

Question: How do you cache complex objects in Spring Boot?
Answer: Ensure objects are serializable and use a caching provider that supports object serialization.

Question: How do you debug caching issues in Spring Boot?
Answer: Enable cache-related logging, use Actuator endpoints, or integrate with profiling tools for detailed insights.

Online Resources

	Practice Paper	YouTube Video Playlist Link
Link	https://forms.gle/pz5cTmGhH6c3Z4MK7	https://www.youtube.com/playlist?list=PLzlh_31VWEFqDZjADGB6Qv7N_VyGpuzXh
QR Code		

CHAPTER 15
Advanced Web Services and Messaging

15.1 RESTful Web Services

Question: What is the @RestController annotation?
Answer: @RestController combines @Controller and @ResponseBody, simplifying the creation of RESTful controllers.

Question: How do you implement custom headers in REST responses?
Answer: Use the ResponseEntity object or the HttpServletResponse object to add custom headers.

Question: What is the use of @RequestHeader?
Answer: @RequestHeader retrieves specific headers from the HTTP request for processing.

Question: How do you handle large file uploads in REST?
Answer: Use MultipartFile in Spring Boot and configure maximum file size in application.properties.

Question: How do you test RESTful services?
Answer: Use tools like Postman, Swagger UI, or automated test frameworks like JUnit with MockMvc.

Question: What is the OPTIONS method in REST?
Answer: The OPTIONS method returns supported HTTP methods for a resource.

Question: What is the difference between PUT and POST?
Answer: PUT updates or creates a resource at a specified URI, while POST creates a new resource under a parent resource.

Question: How do you cache REST responses?
Answer: Use HTTP cache headers like Cache-Control or tools like Redis for server-side caching.

Question: What is the PATCH method used for?
Answer: The PATCH method applies partial updates to a resource.

Question: How do you handle concurrency in RESTful services?
Answer: Use techniques like optimistic locking with versioning fields in the database.

Question: What are the advantages of RESTful web services?
Answer: RESTful services are lightweight, scalable, and use standard HTTP methods for easy integration.

Question: What is a REST API client?
Answer: A REST API client is a software component that interacts with RESTful services using HTTP requests.

Question: How do you implement rate limiting in REST?
Answer: Use tools like API gateways or middleware to restrict the number of API calls from a client.

Question: What is the purpose of the @JsonIgnore annotation?
Answer: @JsonIgnore prevents specific fields from being serialized or deserialized in JSON responses.

Question: How do you handle validation in RESTful services?
Answer: Use validation annotations like @NotNull, @Size, or @Pattern in model classes and handle violations with @ControllerAdvice.

Question: What is the purpose of @Produces and @Consumes annotations?

Answer: These annotations define the media types that a RESTful service can produce or consume.

Question: How do you handle asynchronous requests in REST?
Answer: Use asynchronous processing with CompletableFuture or reactive programming with Spring WebFlux.

Question: What is the use of @RequestMapping?
Answer: @RequestMapping maps HTTP requests to specific controller methods, supporting flexible URI and method configurations.

Question: What is a RESTful URI?
Answer: A RESTful URI uniquely identifies a resource and is designed to be readable and hierarchical.

Question: What is the role of middleware in RESTful services?
Answer: Middleware handles cross-cutting concerns like authentication, logging, and error handling for REST APIs.

15.2 Implementing RESTful Web Services in Java

Question: How do you consume an external RESTful API in Java?
Answer: Use the RestTemplate or WebClient to make HTTP calls to external APIs.

Question: How do you implement HATEOAS in Java REST?
Answer: Use Spring HATEOAS to add links in API responses, guiding clients on available actions.

Question: How do you handle large datasets in RESTful services?
Answer: Implement pagination or streaming to return data in manageable chunks.

Question: How do you cache RESTful API responses?
Answer: Use HTTP caching headers (Cache-Control) or integrate server-side caching with Redis or Ehcache.

Question: What is the purpose of the @RequestHeader annotation?
Answer: It binds specific HTTP headers from the request to method parameters.

Question: How do you test RESTful services in Java?
Answer: Use tools like Postman for manual testing or JUnit with MockMvc for automated testing.

Question: How do you handle concurrency in RESTful services?
Answer: Use optimistic locking with versioning or distributed locks for shared resources.

Question: How do you implement file downloads in RESTful services?
Answer: Return the file as a byte array with appropriate content-type headers in the response.

Question: What is the OPTIONS method used for in REST?
Answer: It retrieves the HTTP methods supported by a specific resource or endpoint.

Question: How do you implement a search feature in a RESTful service?
Answer: Use query parameters to accept search criteria and dynamically construct database queries.

Question: How do you validate JSON input in Spring Boot?
Answer: Use the @Valid annotation in the controller and apply validation annotations in the request model.

Question: How do you handle partial updates in REST?
Answer: Use the HTTP PATCH method to apply partial updates to a resource.

Question: How do you log API calls in RESTful services?
Answer: Use an interceptor or AOP to log request and response details.

Question: How do you implement rate limiting in Java REST?
Answer: Use filters or middleware to restrict the number of API calls per client within a time window.

Question: How do you handle complex nested resources in REST?
Answer: Use hierarchical URIs or flatten the structure with query parameters for better readability.

Question: How do you set up asynchronous REST calls?
Answer: Use CompletableFuture or Spring WebFlux to handle non-blocking asynchronous requests.

Question: How do you implement custom error responses in REST?
Answer: Use @ExceptionHandler to catch exceptions and return detailed error objects.

Question: What is the difference between @RestController and @Controller?
Answer: @RestController combines @Controller and @ResponseBody, simplifying RESTful API development.

Question: How do you parse request parameters from URLs?
Answer: Use @RequestParam for query parameters or @PathVariable for path parameters.

Question: How do you integrate REST with databases in Java?
Answer: Use Spring Data JPA or JDBC to fetch data and return it in RESTful responses.

15.3 Building RESTful Services in Java

Question: How do you handle rate limiting in RESTful services?
Answer: Use API gateways or libraries like Bucket4j to implement rate-limiting mechanisms.

Question: What is the difference between PUT and PATCH in RESTful services?
Answer: PUT replaces the entire resource, while PATCH applies partial updates.

Question: How do you cache responses in RESTful services?
Answer: Use HTTP headers like Cache-Control or implement server-side caching with tools like Redis.

Question: How do you handle asynchronous requests in RESTful services?
Answer: Use CompletableFuture or reactive programming with Spring WebFlux.

Question: What is content negotiation in RESTful services?
Answer: Content negotiation allows clients to specify the desired response format (e.g., JSON, XML) using Accept headers.

Question: How do you implement custom error messages in REST?
Answer: Use @ControllerAdvice and return error objects with detailed messages and codes.

Question: How do you log API calls in RESTful services?
Answer: Use interceptors or Aspect-Oriented Programming (AOP) to log request and response details.

Question: How do you implement request validation in REST?
Answer: Use validation annotations and the @Valid annotation to enforce constraints on input data.

Question: How do you enable Cross-Origin Resource Sharing (CORS) in RESTful APIs?
Answer: Use the @CrossOrigin annotation or configure CORS globally in the WebSecurityConfig class.

Question: How do you integrate RESTful services with databases?
Answer: Use Spring Data JPA or JDBC to interact with the database and return results in REST responses.

Question: How do you implement bulk operations in RESTful APIs?
Answer: Accept lists of resources in the request body and process them iteratively or in batch.

Question: How do you version RESTful APIs?
Answer: Use URI versioning (/v1/resource), header versioning (Accept-Version), or query parameter versioning (?version=1).

Question: How do you handle partial updates in REST?
Answer: Use the HTTP PATCH method and a DTO to apply only the provided changes.

Question: How do you handle nested resources in RESTful services?
Answer: Use hierarchical URIs like /users/{userId}/orders/{orderId} for nested resources.

Question: How do you implement HATEOAS in Spring Boot?
Answer: Use Spring HATEOAS library to add hypermedia links to RESTful responses.

Question: How do you optimize performance in RESTful services?
Answer: Use caching, database indexing, and compression (e.g., Gzip) to enhance performance.

Question: How do you return static files in RESTful services?
Answer: Place static files in the src/main/resources/static folder and serve them directly via HTTP.

Question: How do you implement role-based access control (RBAC) in RESTful services?
Answer: Use Spring Security to assign roles and secure endpoints with @PreAuthorize annotations.

Question: How do you handle timeouts in RESTful services?
Answer: Configure timeouts for the server and client using properties like server.connection-timeout.

Question: How do you consume external RESTful APIs in Java?
Answer: Use RestTemplate or WebClient to perform HTTP operations on external REST APIs.

15.4 Java Message Service (JMS)

Question: What is a JMS Message?
Answer: It is an object that contains the data to be transferred and metadata about the message.

Question: What are the types of JMS messages?
Answer: Types include TextMessage, ObjectMessage, BytesMessage, StreamMessage, and MapMessage.

Question: How do you send a TextMessage in JMS?
Answer: Use session.createTextMessage(String text) and pass it to the MessageProducer.send(Message message) method.

Question: What is the use of JMS Message Selectors?
Answer: Message selectors filter messages based on property values using SQL-like syntax.

Question: How do you set properties in a JMS message?
Answer: Use the setStringProperty(), setIntProperty(), or similar methods on the Message object.

Question: How do you retrieve message properties in JMS?
Answer: Use methods like getStringProperty() or getIntProperty() on the Message object.

Question: How do you handle exceptions in JMS?
Answer: Catch JMSException and implement error-handling logic such as retries or logging.

Question: How do you monitor JMS queues?
Answer: Use management tools provided by the JMS provider, such as JMX in ActiveMQ.

Question: What is the difference between persistent and non-persistent delivery in JMS?
Answer: Persistent delivery ensures messages are not lost during broker failures, while non-persistent delivery does not.

Question: How do you set a message to persistent delivery?
Answer: Call MessageProducer.setDeliveryMode(DeliveryMode.PERSISTENT).

Question: What is a JMS redelivery policy?
Answer: A redelivery policy defines how the JMS provider retries delivering a message after a failure.

Question: How do you implement a message listener in JMS?
Answer: Implement the javax.jms.MessageListener interface and register it with a consumer.

Question: What is the difference between synchronous and asynchronous messaging in JMS?
Answer: Synchronous messaging uses receive() for blocking calls, while asynchronous messaging uses MessageListener.

Question: What is the role of Connection.start() in JMS?
Answer: It begins the delivery of messages to consumers.

Question: How do you stop a JMS connection?
Answer: Call the Connection.stop() method to temporarily stop message delivery.

Question: How do you clean up JMS resources?
Answer: Close the Session, Connection, and other JMS objects in a finally block or use try-with-resources.

Question: How do you configure message priority in JMS?
Answer: Set the priority level using MessageProducer.send(Message message, int priority).

Question: What is a dead letter queue in JMS?
Answer: It is a queue where undeliverable or expired messages are sent for further analysis.

Question: How do you set a time-to-live for JMS messages?
Answer: Use MessageProducer.send() with the time-to-live parameter to specify message expiration.

Question: How do you test JMS messaging?
Answer: Use mock frameworks, integration tests with embedded brokers, or tools like JUnit and ActiveMQ for testing.

15.5 JMS API and Messaging Domains

Question: How do you enable transactions in a JMS session?
Answer: Create the session with the SESSION_TRANSACTED mode.

Question: What are the types of messages in JMS?
Answer: Types include TextMessage, ObjectMessage, BytesMessage, StreamMessage, and MapMessage.

Question: How do you send a TextMessage in JMS?
Answer: Use session.createTextMessage(String text) and pass it to the producer’s send() method.

Question: What are message selectors in JMS?
Answer: Message selectors filter messages using SQL-like conditions on message properties.

Question: What is the purpose of MessageProducer.setDeliveryMode()?
Answer: It sets the delivery mode to persistent or non-persistent.

Question: What is a persistent delivery mode in JMS?
Answer: Persistent mode ensures that messages are stored and not lost during a broker failure.

Question: What is the purpose of Message.setJMSExpiration()?
Answer: It sets the time-to-live for a message, after which it expires.

Question: How do you create a transactional session in JMS?
Answer: Pass true to the Session creation method as the first parameter.

Question: What is the difference between P2P and Pub/Sub?
Answer: P2P (Point-to-Point) delivers messages to a single consumer, while Pub/Sub (Publish-Subscribe) broadcasts messages to multiple subscribers.

Question: What is a JMS message header?
Answer: A message header contains metadata such as JMSDestination, JMSPriority, and JMSExpiration.

Question: How do you use a message selector in JMS?
Answer: Provide a filter string when creating a consumer, e.g., Session.createConsumer(queue, "priority > 5").

Question: What is a dead-letter queue in JMS?
Answer: A queue where undeliverable or expired messages are stored.

Question: What is the role of the Session.commit() method?
Answer: It commits a transaction in a transactional session.

Question: How do you enable asynchronous message delivery?
Answer: Register a MessageListener with a consumer.

Question: What is the purpose of the Connection.start() method?
Answer: It starts the delivery of messages to consumers.

Question: How do you handle exceptions in JMS?
Answer: Catch JMSException and implement retry or fallback mechanisms.

Question: How do you test JMS messaging?
Answer: Use tools like JUnit, ActiveMQ, or embedded brokers for testing.

Question: How do you configure message priority in JMS?
Answer: Set the priority level when sending messages using the send() method.

Question: What is the role of the JMSContext interface?
Answer: Introduced in JMS 2.0, it simplifies connection, session, and producer/consumer management.

Question: How do you monitor JMS queues?
Answer: Use the broker's management console or JMX tools for monitoring queues and topics.

15.6 Design Patterns in Java

Question: What is the Flyweight pattern?
Answer: The Flyweight pattern reduces memory usage by sharing common parts of objects instead of duplicating them.

Question: What is the MVC pattern?
Answer: The Model-View-Controller pattern separates an application into three components: Model (data), View (UI), and Controller (logic).

Question: What is the Front Controller pattern?
Answer: The Front Controller pattern provides a single point of control for handling requests in a web application.

Question: How is the DAO pattern used in Java?
Answer: The Data Access Object (DAO) pattern abstracts persistence logic, separating database operations from business logic.

Question: What is the Dependency Injection (DI) pattern?
Answer: DI provides objects that a class depends on, instead of the class creating them, enhancing modularity and testability.

Question: What is the State pattern?
Answer: The State pattern allows an object to alter its behavior when its internal state changes.

Question: What is the Interpreter pattern?
Answer: The Interpreter pattern defines a representation for a grammar and interprets sentences in the language.

Question: How does the Iterator pattern work?
Answer: The Iterator pattern provides a way to access elements of a collection sequentially without exposing its underlying structure.

Question: What is the Builder pattern's advantage?
Answer: The Builder pattern separates object construction from its representation, enabling complex object creation.

Question: How is the Factory Method pattern implemented?
Answer: Define an interface for creating objects and let subclasses decide which class to instantiate.

Question: What is the Bridge pattern?
Answer: The Bridge pattern separates an abstraction from its implementation, allowing them to vary independently.

Question: What is the purpose of the Visitor pattern?
Answer: The Visitor pattern separates algorithms from the objects they operate on by moving the logic into visitor classes.

Question: What is the Facade pattern?
Answer: The Facade pattern provides a simplified interface to a complex subsystem.

Question: How do you implement the Singleton pattern with thread safety?
Answer: Use synchronized blocks or the Bill Pugh Singleton Design to ensure thread safety.

Question: What is the Null Object pattern?
Answer: The Null Object pattern provides a default behavior instead of null checks, avoiding NullPointerExceptions.

Question: How does the Service Locator pattern work?
Answer: It provides a centralized registry to obtain instances of services, improving lookup performance.

Question: What is the Business Delegate pattern?
Answer: The Business Delegate pattern abstracts the complexity of business services, reducing coupling between clients and services.

Question: What is the Application Controller pattern?
Answer: It centralizes request handling logic for managing workflows in an application.

Question: How does the Lazy Initialization pattern work?
Answer: Lazy Initialization delays the creation of an object until it is needed, saving resources.

Question: What is the Singleton pattern's main disadvantage?
Answer: Singleton introduces global state, making it harder to test and maintain.

15.7 Applying Design Patterns in Java Applications

Question: How is the Bridge pattern used in Java?
Answer: It decouples abstraction and implementation, enabling independent changes, e.g., JDBC drivers.

Question: How is the Visitor pattern used in Java applications?
Answer: It is applied in compilers or XML parsers to perform operations on nodes in a data structure.

Question: What is a real-world use of the Interpreter pattern?
Answer: It is used in scripting engines or regular expression evaluators to parse and execute scripts.

Question: How is the Null Object pattern applied in Java?
Answer: It provides default behavior, avoiding null checks, e.g., returning a default implementation of an interface.

Question: What is the Service Locator pattern used for?
Answer: It centralizes service lookups, improving performance in applications with multiple service layers.

Question: How is the Lazy Initialization pattern used?
Answer: It defers object creation until needed, commonly used in Singleton implementations or Hibernate proxies.

Question: How is the Front Controller pattern applied in web applications?
Answer: It centralizes request handling in frameworks like Spring MVC using a DispatcherServlet.

Question: What is the Application Controller pattern?
Answer: It centralizes control flow and business logic, improving reusability in enterprise applications.

Question: How is the State pattern used in real-world applications?
Answer: It is used in applications like vending machines, where object behavior changes based on state.

Question: How does the Builder pattern improve Test-Driven Development (TDD)?
Answer: It simplifies object creation, making test data setup easier and more maintainable.

Question: How is the Interpreter pattern used in data conversion?
Answer: It translates expressions into SQL queries, making it useful in ORMs or query builders.

Question: How is the Template Method pattern used in testing?
Answer: It defines a sequence of test steps, allowing subclasses to override specific test behavior.

Question: How does the Proxy pattern improve security?
Answer: It controls access to sensitive objects, adding authentication or logging layers.

Question: What is the role of the Observer pattern in microservices?
Answer: It is used in event-driven architectures to notify services of state changes.

Question: How is the Factory pattern applied in dependency injection?
Answer: It creates dependencies dynamically based on runtime conditions in IoC containers.

Question: How does the Adapter pattern support legacy systems?
Answer: It enables legacy components to integrate with modern APIs without altering the original code.

Question: How is the Strategy pattern applied in machine learning?
Answer: It allows dynamic switching of algorithms, such as classification or regression strategies.

Question: What is the benefit of using the Decorator pattern in REST APIs?
Answer: It adds features like authentication or logging dynamically without modifying core logic.

Question: How is the Chain of Responsibility pattern applied in middleware?
Answer: It processes requests through a chain of handlers, such as authentication, logging, or validation middleware.

Question: How is the Composite pattern used in user interfaces?
Answer: It represents UI components hierarchically, enabling uniform treatment of individual and composite widgets.

15.8 Microservices Architecture and Implementation

Question: What is eventual consistency in microservices?
Answer: Eventual consistency ensures that all services have consistent data after a certain period, even in distributed systems.

Question: How do microservices handle database communication?
Answer: Each microservice often uses its own database, ensuring loose coupling and adherence to the database-per-service pattern.

Question: What is the role of DevOps in microservices?
Answer: DevOps practices like CI/CD, infrastructure automation, and monitoring are critical for efficient microservices deployment.

Question: How do microservices handle cross-cutting concerns?
Answer: Cross-cutting concerns like logging, monitoring, and authentication are managed using shared libraries or a service mesh.

Question: What is a service mesh in microservices?
Answer: A service mesh is a dedicated infrastructure layer for handling service-to-service communication, e.g., Istio or Linkerd.

Question: How do you deploy microservices in a cloud environment?
Answer: Use container orchestration tools like Kubernetes along with cloud platforms like AWS, Azure, or Google Cloud.

Question: What are some best practices for microservices development?
Answer: Best practices include defining clear boundaries, implementing CI/CD, and using centralized monitoring tools.

Question: How do you implement retries in microservices?
Answer: Implement retries using libraries like Resilience4j or by configuring retry mechanisms in the API gateway.

Question: What is a distributed trace in microservices?
Answer: Distributed tracing tracks requests across multiple microservices, helping diagnose bottlenecks and failures.

Question: How is load balancing achieved in microservices?
Answer: Load balancing is done using tools like NGINX, HAProxy, or built-in mechanisms in cloud platforms.

Question: What is a circuit breaker in microservices?
Answer: A circuit breaker prevents cascading failures by stopping requests to a failing service.

Question: How does Spring Boot simplify microservices development?
Answer: Spring Boot provides pre-configured tools like Eureka, Feign, and Actuator for quick development and monitoring.

Question: What is API versioning in microservices?
Answer: API versioning allows backward compatibility, supporting multiple API versions for different clients.

Question: What is the role of gRPC in microservices?
Answer: gRPC is a high-performance, lightweight protocol for inter-service communication using Protocol Buffers.

Question: What is the significance of idempotency in microservices?
Answer: Idempotency ensures that multiple identical requests have the same effect, preventing unintended side effects.

Question: How do you secure communication between microservices?
Answer: Use mTLS (mutual TLS), encrypted channels, and API keys for secure inter-service communication.

Question: What is Blue-Green deployment in microservices?
Answer: Blue-Green deployment reduces downtime by switching traffic between two environments during deployment.

Question: How do you manage dependencies between microservices?
Answer: Use event-driven architectures or service registries to manage dependencies dynamically.

Question: What is chaos engineering in microservices?
Answer: Chaos engineering tests system resilience by injecting faults to simulate real-world failures.

Question: How do you design for failure in microservices?
Answer: Use fault-tolerant patterns like retries, circuit breakers, and fallbacks, combined with robust monitoring and alerting.

15.9 Implementing Microservices in Java

Question: How do you enable distributed tracing in Spring Boot?
Answer: Use Spring Cloud Sleuth with Zipkin or Jaeger for distributed tracing.

Question: How do you deploy Java microservices on Kubernetes?
Answer: Package microservices as Docker containers and deploy them using Kubernetes YAML configurations.

Question: What is the role of Helm in deploying microservices?
Answer: Helm simplifies Kubernetes deployments by managing configuration and dependencies using Helm charts.

Question: How do you manage inter-service communication in Java microservices?
Answer: Use REST, gRPC, or event-driven messaging systems like Kafka or RabbitMQ.

Question: What is the purpose of Spring Data JPA in microservices?
Answer: Spring Data JPA simplifies database interactions using repositories and query methods.

Question: How do you handle database migrations in Java microservices?
Answer: Use tools like Flyway or Liquibase for database version control and migrations.

Question: How do you test Java microservices?
Answer: Use unit testing with JUnit, integration testing with TestContainers, and contract testing with Pact.

Question: What is a health check in Java microservices?
Answer: Health checks verify the availability and readiness of a service, often exposed via /actuator/health.

Question: How do you configure a health check endpoint in Spring Boot?
Answer: Enable Spring Boot Actuator and expose health check endpoints in the application.properties file.

Question: What is the purpose of the @LoadBalanced annotation in Spring Boot?
Answer: It enables client-side load balancing using Ribbon.

Question: What is a fault-tolerant design in microservices?
Answer: Fault-tolerant design ensures continued operation during partial service failures using retries, timeouts, and fallbacks.

Question: What is the importance of idempotency in microservices?
Answer: Idempotency ensures that repeated requests produce the same result, preventing data duplication.

Question: How do you handle secrets management in Java microservices?
Answer: Use tools like AWS Secrets Manager, HashiCorp Vault, or Kubernetes Secrets for secure secrets management.

Question: What is Blue-Green Deployment in microservices?
Answer: It minimizes downtime by maintaining two environments (Blue and Green) and switching traffic between them.

Question: How do you implement retries in Spring Boot?
Answer: Use Resilience4j's @Retry annotation or configure retries in the API gateway.

Question: What is a service mesh in microservices?
Answer: A service mesh manages service-to-service communication, security, and monitoring, e.g., Istio.

Question: How do you implement logging in Java microservices?
Answer: Use centralized logging tools like the ELK stack or Splunk and frameworks like Logback or SLF4J.

Question: How do you handle dependencies between microservices?
Answer: Use asynchronous messaging, service registries, or shared contracts via OpenAPI or Swagger.

Question: What is a distributed cache in microservices?
Answer: A distributed cache like Redis or Memcached improves performance by caching frequently accessed data.

Question: How do you secure communication between microservices?
Answer: Use HTTPS, mTLS, and API gateways with OAuth2 or JWT for secure communication.

Online Resources

	Practice Paper	YouTube Video Playlist Link
Link	https://forms.gle/yUFUVbBkzn1xnypV6	https://www.youtube.com/playlist?list=PLzlh_31VWEFpHfA7lPmrp4wpmZYRaA6gU
QR Code		

YouTube Videos Playlists for all Chapters

	CHAPTER 1	CHAPTER 2	CHAPTER 3	CHAPTER 4	CHAPTER 5
Link	https://www.youtube.com/playlist?list=PLzlh_31VWEFrVCJw3kRCEX-irsYWE6lxR	https://www.youtube.com/playlist?list=PLzlh_31VWEFpAiZLj3UJPkHzZrDjgBcgE	https://www.youtube.com/playlist?list=PLzlh_31VWEFpuOaJocdor00sKleSYUmnH	https://www.youtube.com/playlist?list=PLzlh_31VWEFokCbKSWCTyPylh8zmCWzTr	https://www.youtube.com/playlist?list=PLzlh_31VWEFpMZfsWV2xV3X89dvL3CFJd
QR Code					

	CHAPTER 6	CHAPTER 7	CHAPTER 8	CHAPTER 9	CHAPTER 10
Link	https://www.youtube.com/playlist?list=PLzlh_31VWEFrYDrcJYl6fw8TfqdUoi_Q4	https://www.youtube.com/playlist?list=PLzlh_31VWEFrXjFY5rN0-s5xYEApWMbVW	https://www.youtube.com/playlist?list=PLzlh_31VWEFqc1WrGhl0GA26b13vgs3YK	https://www.youtube.com/playlist?list=PLzlh_31VWEFrqnmvicr5j-5aIQOHLGgb7	https://www.youtube.com/playlist?list=PLzlh_31VWEFoytSDG1lrWRVbsPlnvvG3z
QR Code					

	CHAPTER 11	CHAPTER 12	CHAPTER 13	CHAPTER 14	CHAPTER 15
Link	https://www.youtube.com/playlist?list=PLzlh_31VWEFpYOL6QX-brDP98qKT15VMX	https://www.youtube.com/playlist?list=PLzlh_31VWEFqTDh51DnkscBdYCozNemEp	https://www.youtube.com/playlist?list=PLzlh_31VWEFrvrBakYUPoVKhin4X9vhG2	https://www.youtube.com/playlist?list=PLzlh_31VWEFqDZjADGB6Qv7N_VyGpuzXh	https://www.youtube.com/playlist?list=PLzlh_31VWEFpHfA7lPmrp4wpmZYRaA6gU
QR Code					

ABOUT THE BOOK

Java continues to be a dominant programming language in the software industry, powering everything from large-scale enterprise applications to modern cloud-based solutions. With evolving technologies, the demand for Java developers with expertise in Advanced Java concepts has grown significantly.

"Advanced Java for Interviews" is a comprehensive guide designed to help software engineers, students, and professionals strengthen their understanding of core and advanced Java topics while preparing for technical interviews. This book serves as a one-stop resource for Java developers who want to sharpen their knowledge and gain confidence before stepping into an interview. Unlike other Java books that focus purely on theory, this book bridges the gap between theoretical knowledge and practical application. It prepares candidates not just to answer questions but also to think like a Java developer in real-world scenarios. With detailed explanations, code snippets, and best practices, this book will help you gain the confidence needed to excel in any Java interview.

Whether you are preparing for your first Java job or aiming for a senior position, this book will equip you with the knowledge and problem-solving skills required to succeed.